Ava Benny-Morrison has been a journalist since 2009 and is currently *The Sunday Telegraph*'s crime reporter. She has previously worked at *The Sydney Morning Herald and Australian Associated Press*. Ava has won awards for reporting on crime and domestic violence. She grew up in Queensland and currently lives in Sydney. *The Lost Girls* is her first book.

WARNING: THIS BOOK INCLUDES CONTENT RELATED TO SEXUAL ABUSE THAT SOME READERS MAY FIND DISTRESSING.

THE
LOST
AVA BENNY-MORRISON
GIRLS

ABC
BOOKS

The ABC 'Wave' device is a trademark of the
Australian Broadcasting Corporation and is used
under licence by HarperCollins*Publishers* Australia.

HarperCollins*Publishers*
Australia • Brazil • Canada • France • Germany • Holland • Hungary
India • Italy • Japan • Mexico • New Zealand • Poland • Spain • Sweden
Switzerland • United Kingdom • United States of America

First published in Australia in 2019
This edition published in 2020
by HarperCollins*Publishers* Australia Pty Limited
ABN 36 009 913 517
harpercollins.com.au

A catalogue record for this book is available
from the National Library of Australia

ISBN: 978 0 7333 3596 9 (paperback)
ISBN: 978 1 4607 0760 9 (ebook)

Cover design by Darren Holt, HarperCollins Design Studio
Front cover image by Noah Stammbach
Back cover images: Highway in Wynarka, South Australia by Bianca De Marchi/
Newspix; Khandalyce Kiara Pearce by AAP Image/SA Police; Karlie Jade
Pearce-Stevenson by AAP Image/SA Police
Author photo: Tim Hunter/News Corp Australia
Typeset in Bembo Std by Kirby Jones
Printed and bound in Australia by McPherson's Printing Group
The papers used by HarperCollins in the manufacture of this book are a natural,
recyclable product made from wood grown in sustainable plantation forests.
The fibre source and manufacturing processes meet recognised international
environmental standards, and carry certification.

Contents

Part I

Discovery

Chapter 1

The suburban sprawl and housing estates of Sydney's southwestern fringe began to thin as Emmett Hudson and his brother, Dave, powered down the Hume Highway in their car, two dirt bikes in the attached trailer.

They approached the Pheasants Nest service station, where truck drivers on the well-worn Sydney–Canberra route gathered around the outdoor picnic tables and sipped coffee during early morning rest stops. But after a glance at the time, Emmett decided to push on. Without any stops, they'd reach their destination, Belanglo State Forest, at about 10 am.

The winter sun cast a glow over the rolling paddocks rushing past his driver's side window. The four-lane highway was all but deserted on that clear August morning in 2010. It was Emmett's second trip to the forest, which wasn't far from Goulburn and about ninety kilometres inland from the coast. Now thirty-one, he'd been riding motorbikes since he was a kid, just like Dave. The pair lived near Liverpool in Sydney's southwestern suburbs. Monday to Friday was spent working at Dave's restoration business, and their weekend trail rides were usually spent in the Blue Mountains, west of the city.

This time, though, on the urging of mates, they decided to make the hour-and-a-quarter drive south and spend their Sunday on the forest's web of fire trails and narrow, snaking tracks.

Belanglo State Forest is nestled on the western outskirts of the picturesque Southern Highlands, centred around the quaint country towns of Bowral, where French-inspired boutiques and patisseries line the main street, and Berrima, where day trippers wander past charming, colonial-style sandstone buildings.

But the forest has little of that country charm. Most people can tell you about the grim past of the place before they can point to its location on a map. It's notorious as the hunting ground for the infamous serial killer Ivan Milat — a trigger-happy road worker who slaughtered and dumped seven innocent backpackers in the late 1980s and early 1990s.

Emmett knew this, but it didn't deter him. Belanglo was one of Sydney's closest legal dirt bike riding spots.

Now, as he turned off the Hume Highway onto Belanglo Road just before 10 am, he noticed that the farmland on either side of the road was dry. As the bitumen turned to dirt, rutted by the forestry trucks that travelled through every day, Emmett slowed down. He caught a quick glimpse of rusting sheds and rickety homesteads as the pine cover thickened and the sign to Belanglo State Forest appeared.

Motorbike tracks were visible as the route turned into Bunnigalore Road. Eventually, the canopy cover in the southern pocket of the forest became sparse, and sprouting eucalypts bridged the gaps between ironbarks and grey gums.

The grass was long in some spots and cleared in others — it looked as though a fire had torn through some months ago.

Emmett and Dave at last reached the camping ground and pulled over. They were well within the forest boundaries but the distant hum of machinery reminded them civilisation wasn't too far away. Five other riders were already there. Emmett recognised some of them, including his friend Nathan, but there were a couple of fresh faces too. Ten minutes later, three more riders arrived.

After unloading their bikes, they suited up, pulled on their helmets and tightened the straps. Emmett swung his leg over his bike and pushed the clutch in. The engine roared, piercing the still forest air.

They rode off in a plume of dust, traversing the twists and turns of the dirt roads. The brothers hadn't navigated this track before, so Nathan was in the lead. They followed the 'corner man' system, where the leader of the group determines the route, and, when they turn a corner, one rider stays put so those at the back of the pack know where to turn.

Emmett was tearing down the Red Arm Creek Firetrail when he spotted an orange bike stopped at a corner. He turned left and rode for ten or twenty metres before realising that no one was behind him.

'Shit.' He scanned the terrain, looking for a place to turn around. There, in front, he spotted a clearing between a few trees. He slowed his pace to a crawl, keeping an eye out for logs and rocks.

An unusual object on the dark soil of the forest floor caught his eye. Emmett kicked the stand, steadied the bike and jumped off. The object was a bone, a large one, about forty to fifty centimetres long. He crouched down, picked it

up and turned it slowly in his hand. Then, waving the bone
above his head, he called out to his fellow riders. Soon Dave
and another rider, Geoff, appeared. They parked their bikes
and studied the bone curiously, then walked around the site
carefully, looking for other bones. Another smaller bone lay
about three metres away. And another.

'I think it's a pelvic bone,' Geoff said, joining what
appeared to be a femur bone to a larger bone on the ground.
'See how it rotates like a hip joint,' he remarked, slowly
turning the bone ninety degrees.

'Are you a doctor?' Emmett asked.

'No mate, a chiropractor. I'm familiar with bones,' Geoff
replied.

The rest of the riders had come to see what was taking
them so long. One rider peered at the bones on the ground
and shrugged. 'Probably from a kangaroo,' he said bluntly.

'Yeah.' Emmett nodded in cautious agreement, but there
was a tone of unease in his voice. He left the bones on the
ground, the hard white surface a stark contrast to the soft
hues of the fallen leaves on the forest floor.

Having decided the bones belonged to some sort of
animal, the group decided to leave them where they were,
and returned to their cars for lunch. As they refuelled on
sandwiches they discussed their ride, the conversation light
and positive, the adrenalin still flowing.

But the discovery in the forest niggled Emmett. He
wondered whether the bone did belong to an animal; he
thought it was too big.

Dave was having similar thoughts. A few months earlier
he'd read *Sins of the Brother*, a book that detailed the horrific
murders Ivan Milat had carried out in the very forest they
were in. Milat had indiscriminately picked up backpackers

hitchhiking on the desolate highways of the Southern Highlands and taken them to the forest, where he'd murdered then dumped them. The bodies of his seven victims were found at different times. Some had been blindfolded and shot at point blank range. One had been stabbed so ferociously her spinal cord was severed. Dave remembered reading how Milat had hid his victims' bodies under tree logs.

Back riding the tracks after lunch, the dirt bike riders ended up stopping again near the spot where Emmett had found the bones. While the other riders waited at the corner, Dave returned to the clearing where his brother had made the discovery hours earlier. The leaves crunched as his tyres slowly rolled over the dry ground. Not sure what he might find, his eyes were peeled and his heart thumped.

Dave spotted the bones they'd seen earlier, then a fallen tree log caught his eye. The hollow log was blackened and peeling. Dave's eyes fixed on something and his stomach flipped. He felt his mouth become dry. Poking out of the ground, surrounded by twigs and pale gumnut leaves, was a human skull.

With a sense of alarm in his voice, Dave called out to Emmett and the other riders. 'There's a skull.'

A few centimetres from the skull, in a neat pile, as if a barber had swept up his salon floor at the end of the day, was a clump of light, ginger-coloured hair. Nearby, in a scattered heap, lay a pile of long, curved bones. Some were snapped or black, scarred by the flames of a bushfire, perhaps, but they looked like rib bones. Teeth jutted out of a jawbone sitting on top of the foliage about a metre from the skull.

Dave swallowed hard as he tried to comprehend what he'd found. The bones lay in an open clearing, not far from a designated fire trail, a path popular with weekend riders. He wondered how long they'd been lying there unnoticed.

The other riders were now gathered around. Alarmed, they speculated about who the bones might belong to and how they got there. The conversation turned to Ivan Milat. Dave recalled what he'd read in the book and tried to determine whether there were any similarities to the scene in front of him.

The seriousness of their discovery began to dawn on them. They would need to call the police, and probably shouldn't have trampled over what could be a crime scene.

But when they checked their mobile phones, only one of them had reception. He passed the phone to a visibly upset Dave, whose hands shook as he called Bowral Police Station.

When the call came through at the station, the officer on duty asked the caller to text a picture of the bones to the sergeant on duty. Since Milat gave the forest its notorious reputation, it was not unusual for bushwalkers, campers or motorbike riders to call in with claims of having found human remains. Once a clueless bushwalker had even turned up at the station clutching a bone he'd found. More often than not the remains turned out to be animal bones. So to avoid having to send two officers to the forest for no reason, the police preferred to first get a better idea of what they were dealing with.

The sergeant at the station received the photograph in a text message and it was immediately clear that the dirt bike riders had found a human skull. The officer on the phone told the brothers to meet police closer to the entrance of the park, at the camping ground, in about fifteen minutes.

The riders jumped back on their bikes and started the journey out of the forest. The lightness they had felt from the thrill of the day's ride was lost, replaced by uneasiness.

By now the forest had grown darker as the afternoon light began to fade. Emerging from the fire trail, the riders turned onto Brethren Point Road, a track that snaked back towards Bunnigalore Road. Less than one kilometre along, they passed a weatherboard home on a small property squeezed between pine plantations. Cattle grazed the long grass skirting the fence, and someone was tinkering in the open garage. It was a striking contrast to the discovery they'd just made.

When they arrived at the designated spot where they were to meet the police, the riders chatted, but their conversation felt forced, their nervousness apparent. Ten minutes later, a cloud of dust tailing a four-wheel-drive announced the arrival of the police.

Three uniformed officers got out of the car and introduced themselves.

'Can you boys take us in?' one officer asked.

For the third time that day, the brothers returned to the leafy location where the bones lay. They stood back while the constables walked fifteen metres ahead, following Emmett's instructions.

After viewing the skull and other bones, the police officers quickly cordoned off the area with blue and white chequered tape. Now the place in the forest was a crime scene. Standing on the other side of the tape, Emmett and Dave felt the gravity of the situation in which they'd unexpectedly found themselves sink in.

Chapter 2

Detective Senior Constable Bill Dowton was the only detective on shift at Bowral Police Station, so when the call came through that bones had been found in Belanglo State Forest, it became his problem.

Although calls like these were received sporadically each year, this afternoon was different. Three general duties officers who'd been sent out to check the bones called Detective Dowton to confirm that the motorbike riders had indeed stumbled upon part of a human skeleton. So, when he couldn't raise his boss, Detective Sergeant Rod Grant, Dowton had jumped in the police four-wheel-drive and headed west.

As he drove along Oxleys Hill Road in the direction of the forest, he made a mental checklist of what he would have to do: call the crime manager at Goulburn, let the crime scene unit at Wollongong know they'd need examiners out in the forest by sundown; and touch base with the duty officer.

For a moment, his mind turned to Ivan Milat; you couldn't blame him, considering his history with the case. After years working in inner Sydney as a detective, including investigating the murder of renowned heart surgeon Dr Victor Chang, Detective Dowton had escaped the city with his wife and two young daughters to Bowral in 1991.

Ironically, a year later, Dowton found himself on one of Australia's most high-profile and notorious serial killer investigations. He was the first detective called out to Belanglo State Forest after two friends on an orienteering course came across the decomposing body of British backpacker Joanne Walters on 19 September 1992. The knife wounds on her body were a chilling indication that something evil had ended the young woman's life. The following day, the body of another young woman, Caroline Clarke, was found. There were ten bullet holes in her head, as if she'd been lined up and used as target practice.

Over the course of fourteen months, seven bodies were found, and Task Force Air was formed to investigate the mass killings. The area in the forest where the bodies were dumped was searched extensively. Officers used huge sieves to sift through every inch of dirt; sniffer dogs were deployed across a large area; metal detectors scanned the earth and dozens of police were deployed to conduct line search after line search.

Now, as he headed back out to the forest, Dowton's mind turned to those events some eighteen years earlier, and he entertained the possibility that another Milat victim may have been discovered. The bones had been found next to a log, similar to the way Caroline Clarke's body was discovered. However, they'd been found in the southwest corner of the forest, whereas Milat's victims had been clustered in the northern pocket of Belanglo.

One of the first lessons a detective is taught is not to settle on one theory early in an investigation. 'Keeping an open mind' is a term police use regularly; detectives are to assume nothing, believe no one and check everything.

So while Milat occupied his mind, Dowton was already weighing up other theories — murder at the hands of someone else, suicide or misadventure. After thirty-six years in the police force, nothing shocked or surprised him, and he treated the call-out as he would any other job.

Dowton turned off Brethren Point Road onto the Red Arm Creek Firetrail. Three hundred metres along the trail he spotted three uniformed police officers and a few motorbike riders standing near the start of an unnamed track.

Dowton pulled up, stepped out of the car and introduced himself to the motorbike riders.

Dave and Emmett nodded. They seemed dumbstruck.

'Did you find the bones?' Dowton looked at Dave and made a mental note of his age — late twenties probably.

Dave nodded again. One of the uniformed police officers, Sergeant Darren Farr, stepped in and offered to take Dowton for a closer look.

Several metres down the unnamed track was the leg bone. Then, beside a large log, Dowton spotted the skull, vertebrae and a clump of hair. If the skeleton had been in the forest for a while, exposed to the elements and animals, it was no surprise the bones were dispersed.

'Looks like it's been here for several months,' he said, crouching down for a closer look.

Dowton and Farr agreed the scene looked suspicious. The bones had been found next to a fallen log, possibly in an attempt to hide the body, and the location was remote, not somewhere a bushwalker would be likely to come across.

Dowton walked back to the motorbike riders. They appeared shaken up — clearly it had been a long day. 'You blokes are right to go,' he told them. They'd need to provide a statement to police, he said, but they could do it the following day at Liverpool Police Station, closer to home.

Not long after Dave and Emmett had gone, Detective Sergeant Rodney Grant arrived. Like Dowton, he knew the forest well. He'd camped in the woods with his family and negotiated the twisting fire trails on his own motorbike.

Detective Grant noted the skeleton's location next to a fallen tree and acknowledged that it was in a completely different area of the forest to where Milat's victims were found. Then, as the light began to fade, a crime scene officer from Wollongong arrived. The conversation turned to how the scene would be guarded overnight. The fading light presented a challenge: floodlights could only do so much, and without more resources police wouldn't be able to conduct a thorough search anyway. It was decided two general duties officers would stay overnight, more than likely huddled in front of the heater inside a police four-wheel-drive.

At 8:25 pm, Detectives Grant and Dowton left the forest and drove back to Bowral Police Station, where a briefing note was prepared for senior police. The discovery would undoubtedly attract a lot of attention and the detectives were bracing themselves for a big day ahead. The area would need to be searched extensively and every bone photographed and recorded in situ before anything was taken out of the forest for forensic examination. The topsoil, about ten centimetres deep, would need to be sifted to find any missing teeth or other tiny pieces of evidence. This process would likely take days and attract fierce media interest. The NSW Homicide Squad — a specialist unit of one hundred detectives who worked a rotating on-call roster and responded to suspicious deaths around the state — would also be notified.

Usually, the seventy-two-hour window after a crime was committed was crucial: bullet casings could be found in gutters, and guns in bins; witnesses' recollections were still fresh; and DNA could be swabbed from clothing, walls or cars.

But this was not a usual case. Police didn't know how long ago the crime had been committed. Any item bearing evidentiary value could be long gone, swept away by floods, bushfires or scavengers, and it would be extremely difficult to tell if the person had died in Belanglo or somewhere else. Bowral detectives were a tiny team in a quiet country police station, and would need all the help they could get.

* * *

At 9 pm that night, the NSW Police Media Unit issued a brief, five-paragraph statement about the discovery of the bones.

'Goulburn police are investigating the discovery of skeletal remains found in the Belanglo State Forest this afternoon in the Southern Highlands,' read the email, which was sent out to hundreds of journalists and newsrooms across the state.

'About 3:15 pm (Sunday 29 August) a group of trail bike riders discovered a number of bones in the Belanglo State Forest.

'Police were immediately called and secured a crime scene.

'Goulburn detectives along with Wollongong Crime Scene attended and investigations are continuing.

'A search of the area was suspended due to poor lighting and will continue tomorrow morning.'

The mere mention of Belanglo State Forest and bones in the same paragraph had been enough to whip up a media frenzy, and by the following morning, the grim discovery was the leading story on every radio and television bulletin in Sydney. Anticipation was in the air as reporters speculated whether the bones belonged to another of Ivan Milat's victims. Senior reporters peeled off from the media throng to call police contacts, hoping for a nudge in the right direction, but investigators were tight-lipped.

By midmorning, the sky above the forest was abuzz with news helicopters. Aerial access was all the media had — the growing press pack on the ground had been stopped by police tape strung across Brethren Point Road. All the media could see was a police cage truck blocking the entrance to the Red Arm Creek Firetrail.

At the crime scene, forensic officers were placing small yellow, numbered triangles beside each bone on the ground before taking photographs, while a few metres away officers used a sieve to search the topsoil. Nearby, Dowton, Grant and two homicide squad investigators kept an eye on proceedings. The crime scene officers decided how the area should be searched and the detectives chipped in when needed.

They had been at the scene for almost twenty-four hours and still had no idea how long the skeleton had been there. Noting the blackened tree trunks in the area, police asked the Forestry Corporation of New South Wales for information regarding controlled burns over the previous year. The department carried out hazard reduction burn-offs in the forest during the winter months to reduce natural fuels, like dry fallen leaves, ahead of the bushfire season. Records showed a burn had been undertaken in the southern pocket of the forest twelve months prior. Given some of the bones showed signs of fire damage, that suggested they'd been in the forest for at least a year.

Just after 1 pm, Goulburn Local Area Command boss Superintendent Evan Quarmby held a press conference outside Bowral Police Station to satisfy the media interest.

'Very early indications at this stage, which can't be confirmed until the results of a post-mortem, is that the remains appear to be female,' Quarmby told reporters. 'The post-mortem is likely to commence today, or will commence tomorrow. But the results of that will not be known until we conclude the investigation out at the actual crime scene itself. The processing of the actual crime scene is very meticulous, we are being very thorough. We are literally sifting through soil, basically grain by grain ... to make sure we recover everything that is possibly linked to this investigation.'

Superintendent Quarmby paused to take questions from the journalists.

Did police believe it could be Ivan Milat's eighth victim?

'It's early days and far too soon for us to know exactly what's happened,' he answered patiently. 'Obviously there is a lot of speculation surrounding this discovery but we definitely will not be jumping to conclusions.'

The response didn't satisfy the journalists and the questions about Milat kept coming.

Were there any similarities? Had police spoken to Milat yet? Would they speak to him?

The press conference started to go around in circles before Quarmby thanked everyone for coming and walked back inside.

Detective Grant was aware of the relentless Milat speculation but told his team to ignore it. 'Keep an open mind,' he reminded them. Privately, he wondered, *If I was a murderer, where would be the best place to dump a body so someone else got the blame?*

However, despite police attempts to hose down the speculation, Ivan Milat remained a strong theme throughout the day's media coverage.

The police search in the forest lasted three days. During that time, police made a number of significant discoveries that would remain out of the public domain. These included, among the leaves and twigs a few metres from the skeleton, a crumpled T-shirt, its white cotton stained dirt brown. The tattered rag — with a pink love heart motif and the word 'Angelic' printed across it — had been rolled in a ball and had been exposed to the elements for so long it had dried hard. As well, a small, single white sock was found. With delicate, gloved hands, crime scene officers picked up the shirt and the tiny sock and carefully placed them into a brown evidence bag. Remarkably, the T-shirt had not been damaged by fire.

A single silver sleeper earring also turned up as police sifted through the topsoil. The three items suggested the bones belonged to a female.

The bones were transported to the morgue in Glebe. There, the skeleton was laid out on a stainless-steel table, and a forensic pathologist, with guidance from a forensic anthropologist, determined the bones belonged to a female aged between thirteen and twenty-five years old at the time of death. Her body could have been on the forest floor for anywhere between six months and ten years.

It was a wide timeframe and would have implications for how much information, including missing persons records, police would have to sift through. However, it did all but rule out the theory that Milat was involved; he'd been arrested over the backpacker killings in 1994 and had been in jail ever since. If this woman had been killed ten years earlier, in the year 2000, well, Milat was by then already in custody.

The post-mortem examination revealed fractures, almost perfectly aligned, to multiple ribs on both sides of the chest. Punches alone would not have been forceful enough to cause the fractures; the injuries were more consistent with someone coming down on the chest and abdomen with considerable force. If the pressure was enough to crack the woman's ribs, it would have been lethal to her soft organs.

The pathologist formed the opinion that death was caused by 'one or more applications of blunt force to the trunk'. The injuries strongly suggested the application of at least one episode of significant force, perhaps by way of 'forceful stomping or kneeing'.

Chapter 3

Hidden behind high fences, the Forensic and Analytical Science Service Centre (FASS) is a sprawling compound of ageing concrete buildings, the exterior bland and uninviting. Beyond the paint-flecked bars of a dull red fence is a large cemetery. The building barely attracts a glance from motorists travelling on the busy western Sydney road outside. Small signs at the complex entrance instruct visitors to turn down a wide driveway before they reach the first of two intercoms and arrive at the main building; security is paramount.

This is home to New South Wales's only forensic DNA facility. It's where human remains are identified and where police bring cases that require DNA testing to crack. The forensic biologists help put names to unidentified remains and extract faint traces of DNA from tattered pieces of evidence left behind at crime scenes.

Staff play an important part in the criminal investigation process but they're removed from the front line. They're not interviewing suspects or making arrests, but are nevertheless cautious about identifying themselves and their workplace.

They ask that the lab's exact location not be disclosed in media reports and be only vaguely referred to as somewhere in the city's western suburbs.

Within the sterile and decontaminated boundaries of block E, behind their blue scrubs and white facial masks, forensic biologists objectively carry out their jobs with humility and without judgement. But for some, they are part of the police effort to dig up damning evidence and so become part of the prosecution.

One such forensic biologist is Dr David Bruce. The self-confessed technophile has devoted his career to forensic biology. Much of his work has been at FASS, analysing the forensic value of evidence and DNA profiles extracted from unidentified remains or confirming the identities of murder victims.

He speaks about the science with a passion that is both endearing and comforting. Ask him to explain the difference between nuclear and mitochondrial DNA and a schoolboy's smile spreads across his face before he embarks on an eager analysis of the incredibly complex field.

The work of Dr Bruce and his colleagues at FASS has helped solve some of New South Wales' most high-profile criminal cases, but the ones that are never solved stay with him.

Dr Bruce had been about to sit down for dinner on 30 August 2010 when a bulletin about bones found in the Belanglo State Forest flashed across his television screen. The mention of the notorious forest sent him back nearly two decades in time to FASS's involvement in generating DNA profiles from blood samples, muscle tissue and evidence collected from crime scenes as part of the serial killer Ivan Milat investigation. Over a two-year period, small pieces of seven different skeletons made their way to the laboratories, and forensic biologists helped identify those backpackers.

The next morning, a box containing a tibia bone was delivered to the FASS laboratory with a request for a DNA profile generation. The bone was part of a female skeleton found in the Belanglo State Forest. Some of the bones found in the forest had been blackened by fire and could have been in the forest for years. They'd been found scattered across several metres, and were of a woman, aged between thirteen and twenty-five years old.

While Dr Bruce, as a senior forensic biologist, would confirm a DNA match, the job of extracting DNA from the bone would fall to Kara Wilson. Ms Wilson was the only biologist at FASS qualified to extract nuclear DNA from bones, a specialty she'd pursued after changing the course of her career from immunology to forensic biology. She had a keen interest in crime; joining the police force had been a back-up career choice if she couldn't get into university to study science. In 2001, she found a way to combine both passions and started as a forensic biologist at the FASS evidence recovery unit.

At the time DNA was emerging as a powerful tool in solving crimes, and law enforcement had begun to realise its true potential. The Australian Crime Commission (as it was then known) had just set up the National Criminal Investigation DNA Database, a ground-breaking resource that could match DNA profiles from criminals to DNA found at crime scenes. DNA was being used more than ever before to crack cases, linking crimes from one side of the country to a criminal languishing in a jail on the other side, and identifying people who had been missing for decades.

It was an exciting time to work in forensic science and Wilson's job put her in the thick of it. She found fulfilment knowing her work identified missing persons, or 'John and Jane Does', providing answers to their families and helping police pinpoint perpetrators who deserved to be brought to justice.

Now, in her office, Wilson reviewed the documentation detailing the Belanglo case. Given the high-profile nature of the investigation and the fact it was unidentified remains, she assumed there was a sense of urgency.

After collecting the bone from downstairs she returned to her lab and drew down the hood — a piece of clear Perspex with holes to poke her gloved hands through — onto her workbench. The metre-wide divider and inbuilt exhaust fan would protect her from the dust that would plume when she began sanding, sawing and cutting the bone.

The bone had been exposed to the elements but it was in surprisingly good condition. Degradation was minimal, and Wilson was confident she'd be able to extract nuclear DNA, which would then be sent to the DNA processing unit.

The first step was cleaning the bone and then breaking it down into a powder — a tedious, gradual process that took Wilson half a day. It was not like an episode of *CSI*, where the simple press of a button would spit out the identity of who the bone belonged to. The small pieces of bone would then be placed in a cylinder and submerged in liquid nitrogen, which would break the bone down even further into a powder before Wilson could assess how much nuclear DNA there was. Fortunately, in this case there was enough DNA to generate a complete profile.

Like all unidentified persons cases, the profile was immediately uploaded onto the National Criminal Investigation DNA Database. A match could have provided police with a name, a location, or at the very least, a solid lead to pursue, but it gave them nothing. The bones didn't belong to a criminal who had been swabbed for DNA in a police watch house, a clumsy fugitive who'd left traces at a crime scene interstate or a missing person with a profile circulating in the database. It was unlikely that the girl whose remains were found in the Belanglo State Forest had been arrested for a serious crime in any Australian state or territory in recent years.

Instead, had the girl been dead, and her body slowly decaying in the middle of nowhere for years, without anyone noticing she was gone?

The result was frustrating for Wilson, who, like a craftsman proud of their work, had generated a 'beautiful' DNA profile that was at that point, useless. It was also frustrating for homicide squad investigators, who had hoped it would give them a steer in the right direction.

The one catch about the DNA database was that it didn't have the technology to make familial matches: a child's DNA wouldn't automatically match with the mother's DNA profile. That process had to be done manually by a forensic biologist like Ms Wilson.

Immediately after the DNA profile was generated, the NSW Police Missing Persons Unit began selecting cases for comparison.

'I think people don't really appreciate how much police do persevere. They are constantly working on unsolved investigations, as well as whatever else they have in their current case load,' Dr Bruce said later. 'They are always sending samples saying, "Could it possibly be this? Could you compare it with this person?" A lot of the time with missing persons cases it was, "Could this be the daughter of these two individuals?" And that is the only reference material you have.'

Around the same time, the case was assigned to Detective Sergeant Tim Attwood from the NSW Homicide Squad. The squad operated on a seven-day roster with six teams of detectives rotating through on-call periods. They responded to homicides and suspicious deaths around New South Wales and oversaw the first seventy-two hours of every investigation. If the case was straightforward — a husband who'd killed his wife and been arrested at the scene with the murder weapon still in his hand — local detectives would take the lead in the job. If it was complex — a gangland murder with fears of retaliation, or a classic 'whodunnit' — the homicide squad would likely take carriage of the investigation.

In the weeks after the bones were found, Detective Attwood's team compiled a shortlist of dozens of missing persons of a similar age range. The Belanglo State Forest is on the Hume Highway, a major national highway connecting Victoria, New South Wales and the Australian Capital Territory. For that reason, police looked into missing persons records from interstate and included some of those cases on their shortlist.

The NSW Police Forensic Intelligence and Results Management team coordinated the search, sending missing persons profiles to FASS to compare against the DNA profile from the bones found in Belanglo. If there wasn't a DNA profile for the missing person, police would track down a living relative and ask for a sample so it could be examined for a familial comparison. The parents of missing persons agreed to take part in these DNA comparisons, hopeful but still prepared for the likelihood that it wouldn't be their son or daughter.

In New South Wales, police could request a mitochondrial DNA sample from the mother of a person who has been missing for three months. A nuclear DNA sample could also be generated from hair found on a missing person's brush or the bristles of a toothbrush. These samples were then kept as exhibits at the NSW Police Missing Persons Unit. Some of the missing persons on the shortlist hadn't been seen for decades, others were high-profile suspected murder cases, such as that of schoolgirl Quanne Diec. Quanne was twelve years old when she left her home in Granville for Strathfield Girls High School in July 1998 to board the 8:05 am train from Clyde to Strathfield. She never made it.

Rewards of $100,000 and $200,000 for information leading to her whereabouts yielded no result, and in 2010, Quanne was still missing. Her young age put her slightly outside the estimate for the bones in Belanglo, but on the off-chance the anthropologist's assessment was out, a DNA sample from Quanne's mother was used for a comparison.

In a couple of hours, Kara Wilson knew the bones did not belong to the missing schoolgirl, an undeniably disappointing outcome. She felt as though she had to break the news of another non-match every other week. The more names police crossed off the shortlist, the more they wondered what had been missed or overlooked.

Investigators needed to know who the girl was and why no one had reported her missing.

Chapter 4

To the sound of clicking cameras, NSW Homicide Squad boss, Detective Superintendent Peter Cotter, strode to the podium. It was 15 September 2010 and Sydney's media had been called to the State Crime Command in Parramatta for an update on the Strike Force Hixson investigation.

It had been a fortnight since any significant update on the investigation and there was a feverish sense of anticipation among reporters in the room, some of whom had stood around Belanglo State Forest for days covering the story when it first broke. The journalists chatted among themselves, sharing theories and bits of background information gleaned from police sources.

In a strategic move, investigators hadn't spoken publicly about the clothing found with the bones on 29 August. They'd wanted to hold back the information in case it was needed for a public appeal down the track, and as a way of reinvigorating interest in the case.

Two weeks devoted to extensive DNA testing and methodically scouring missing persons records hadn't thrown up any solid leads. Outside of a DNA profile, the only other identifying feature police had was the unique, size 10 T-shirt. It had taken a couple of days for detectives to track down the origin of the T-shirt's brand — Chain Reaction for Girls — to a manufacturer in China. The mass-produced T-shirt had been sold in Australia between 2003 and 2006, and the assumption was that someone would have purchased the same clothing and, with a subtle reminder, would remember where from. If police knew what store sold the T-shirt, they would be able to investigate that location in case the girl lived locally.

Investigators on the strike force decided to release an artist's impression of the T-shirt in the hope someone would recognise it. Detectives thought releasing a photograph of the T-shirt seemed distasteful and, given it had been exposed to elements in the forest for so long, the fabric was extremely delicate. The idea was to avoid cross-contaminating the T-shirt with other DNA profiles while forensic officers were still trying to pick up any identifying traces.

Instead, an officer at the crime scene unit sketched an artist's impression from a photograph of the T-shirt, carefully illustrating the hot pink stitching around the neckline, the rose, love heart and wings that made up the motif, and the pink cursive letters that spelled the word 'Angelic'. It would be the first time anyone outside the tight team of detectives working on the case would hear about what else had been found in the Belanglo State Forest in late August.

Detective Cotter shuffled his papers and the room fell quiet.

'We believe the T-shirt has significant importance to the investigation,' he explained as he held up the sketch on a piece of A4 paper.

'It's a girl's shirt, size 10, and while it didn't contain any of the skeletal remains, it was found in very close proximity to the main part of the skeleton.'

There were up to thirty missing girls who fitted the age range and timeframe of the case, he added, but police were also entertaining the possibility that the victim could be from overseas. As well, the hope was that, by releasing more details about the young woman, including her T-shirt, it would reassure families of some missing persons that the girl wasn't their loved one.

The new details about the mystery were aired on every news bulletin, generating a lot of interest. Media outlets gravitated towards the word 'Angelic'; it created a new sense of vulnerability and innocence, and the unidentified woman became known as Angel. But while the police received many phone calls, no valuable information was gleaned. Detective Attwood would never find anyone who had bought or owned the same T-shirt, in what became another bizarre aspect of the baffling case.

As the case ticked on without a result, the strike force began to explore unorthodox investigative paths. A forensic orthodontist examined Angel's skull — the upper and lower incisors were missing and others were found scattered on the forest floor — and concluded the girl's teeth showed signs of Western dentistry. In search of the girl's dental records, Detective Attwood contacted dental surgeries in the Bowral area, despite the fact he realised that the girl could have grown up somewhere completely different and had ended up in Belanglo State Forest on her travels. A notice was placed in the *Australian Dental Journal* about the bones and the ambitious hunt for records, but it, too, yielded no results.

With state and nationwide long-term missing persons records exhausted, Detective Attwood began looking overseas for answers. He scoured through Interpol missing persons records looking for young women between thirteen and twenty-five years old who hadn't been seen for years. Immigration records were cross-checked for travellers who had entered Australia on holiday visas and never departed.

The idea that Angel was from another part of the world was supported by a stable isotope analysis, which suggested the bones had chemical markers that were consistent with Angel not having spent much time in Australia. But even then, the analysis was not specific enough that it narrowed down the search to one country. Someone living in Canada may have the same tissue or bone markings as someone in Iran.

Three months after Angel's remains were found, the Belanglo State Forest was thrust into the spotlight again when Ivan Milat's nephew, Matthew Milat, was arrested for killing his teenage friend, David Auchterlonie, with an axe in the forest. Matthew, a meek nineteen-year-old with a mop of curly orange hair, had drawn inspiration from his great uncle, who he hadn't seen since he was a toddler but had developed a sick fascination for as a teenager.

On the night of David's seventeenth birthday, 20 November 2010, Matthew and a friend, Cohen Klein, lured the birthday boy into the forest and slaughtered him with a double-sided axe. David's body was dragged to the roadside and a careless attempt made to cover him with a few tree branches before Matthew took off.

The next day, Matthew boasted about the heinous act. 'You know me, you know my family,' he proudly confessed to a friend. 'You know the last name Milat. I did what they do.'

Another boy who was in the car with Matthew and Klein that night was too shaken up to keep the crime a secret and confessed to his father. Matthew and Klein were arrested a day later.

The case attracted national media attention and drew the interest of Strike Force Hixson investigators, who weighed up the possibility that Matthew Milat was also the killer they were looking for. But he would have been sixteen years old or younger when Angel was killed in the Belanglo State Forest, and detectives eventually ruled him out in another dead end.

Homicide investigations were notoriously gruelling and time-consuming; they required a high level of patience, stamina and determination. But this case was certainly testing the detectives' resolve.

Chapter 5

Dr Susan Hayes had found the text just as she was finishing up presenting a 3D facial-reconstruction workshop at the National Portrait Gallery in Canberra.

Please call NSW homicide.

Her first reaction was to wonder if something had happened to a family member, but given they didn't live in New South Wales, she put that aside. So why would the NSW Homicide Squad want to talk to her?

She made the return call and a Detective Attwood answered. For the past year, he said, he'd been trying to identify a female skeleton found south of Sydney. 'I noticed your work ... We want to know if you could help us create a picture of what she might have looked like,' he asked.

It would be the first time in New South Wales that a facial approximation would be used in a homicide investigation.

Dr Hayes was a forensic anthropologist at the University of Western Australia. Her experience with forensic cases in Australia involved identifying living people and, other than her anatomy studies and intensive training with forensic cases in Europe, her work with skeletal remains had predominantly been with people who had died a long time ago. Her niche field of research had taken her to exotic overseas destinations, studying skulls that were hundreds, sometimes thousands of years old. She'd worked with CT scans to estimate facial appearance, but liked being able to handle a skull in her hands to understand the shapes and create her own story as to how that person had died.

Curious as to how he'd been led to her, she told Attwood that there were other people in her line of work he could approach. 'One of the reasons I moved into archaeology was because of the stories,' she now explained to Detective Attwood. 'Basically, I can imagine that they died in the loving arms of their family.' In forensic cases, a victim's ending was rarely peaceful.

As well, she had a very academic approach to her work, she said. There would be no opinions offered as to who the young woman was or what had happened to her. 'It's very important the person I'm working with understands that I'll do that,' Dr Hayes said. 'And what I do is applied research. It's very careful and so it's a very slow process.'

Detective Attwood said he understood. He would sleep on it and let her know in the morning.

The next day Dr Hayes received an email from Detective Attwood, formally asking her whether she would help create a picture of what the victim may have looked like.

Two weeks later, Dr Hayes and Detective Attwood were greeted by a team of odontologists, pathologists and detectives at Sydney's morgue, located in the belly of the Coroner's Court Complex on Parramatta Road in Glebe. She would be working in a room reserved for murder victims.

'If we don't get a murder overnight you'll be back working in here tomorrow,' Detective Attwood told her matter-of-factly.

Dr Hayes requested that police only provide her with basic but necessary case details: age range, approximate time of death, gender, population affinity, and the location where the bones were found. She wanted to treat the situation like any other clinical case, and further details about how the girl died could impact her objectivity.

She got to work, but used to working in solitude and not under the curious gaze of eager detectives, Hayes' nerves were showing. At one point, Detective Attwood inhaled sharply as, clumsy in her self-consciousness, she fumbled and almost dropped the skull on the tiled floor.

Dr Hayes noted how well preserved and immaculate a condition the bones were in. Her initial focus was getting the jaw to best fit with the skull, as this would guide her as to the shape of the girl's face. The dimensions of the teeth helped estimate the girl's mouth shape. While the lateral incisors were missing — not uncommon with single-rooted teeth that dislodge easily — the rest of the teeth were in place.

The next task was to measure the aspects of the skull. The measurements would also be used to estimate the shape and size of the face, and to check for perspective distortion in the digital photographs on which the face would be based.

Painstakingly and methodically, Dr Hayes measured the jaw width and height, height of the teeth, nasal aperture dimensions and orbital bones. Anatomical locations or 'landmarks' were pinpointed and would be used to gauge soft tissue depths. The skull was then placed on a stand and carefully positioned, checked and checked again, before it was photographed extensively. The images and measurements would aid Dr Hayes when she began the long process of estimating the face.

Back in Perth a week later, the smell of the morgue lingered, the unmistakable musky scent permeating her clothing and hair. Everything she'd taken to Sydney had to be washed, some clothing twice over.

As she worked to recreate the girl's face, Dr Hayes' thoughts would turn to the high school students she taught. They were in their teens, heading into adulthood, getting ready to leave their parents' homes and start their own families and careers. Maybe Angel had been like that too.

The parallel left her unsettled. Hayes didn't want it to distract her from the crucial work she had left to do, crafting the facial approximation based on the calculations she had recorded, and using a computer graphics program to magnify the photographs.

The only thing she couldn't glean from the skull was what the girl's hair may have been like. So, with Detective Attwood's permission, Dr Hayes asked a hairdresser friend, Sally Bowley, to give her a rough idea of the girl's hairstyle. Cuttings from the hair found near the bones in the Belanglo State Forest had been photographed to scale before Dr Hayes left Sydney. From the photographs, Sally concluded the hair was straight, medium length and not bleached or coloured. Based on the approximate age of the young woman, she selected a hairstyle that was popular from that time. It was difficult, though, to assess the texture and mass of the hair — thick or thin — from the photographs alone. Working with the hairdresser's assessment, Dr Hayes created a style that was layered, shoulder length and with a long side fringe.

Finally, weeks later, Dr Hayes stared back at the computerised image of the girl's face she had estimated:

wide-set eyes, a full face, thin lips, a small mouth and a wide jaw. The girl's nose dominated her soft face and a fringe swept across her forehead.

Based on feedback from the forensic team back at the morgue, Dr Hayes made some adjustments. Finally, after many hours scrutinising the bone shapes and measurements, and dozens of emails back and forth with Detective Attwood, Dr Hayes was content with the result.

It was a strange feeling looking at the girl's face. Hayes wondered about the girl's parents and friends, where they might be and whether they still thought she was alive. There was a strange sense of intimacy in her work, and it instilled in Dr Hayes a duty to be as thorough, respectful and caring as possible, to represent the girl as best she could.

When she'd agreed to work on the case with New South Wales Police, she said she didn't want to be paid for the work, she only wanted to use the experience for a research paper. Dr Hayes treated the case objectively and separated the emotion from it, but the uniqueness and trauma was not lost on her. In the months after she finished the project, she walked through the supermarket and thought she spotted the girl in one of the aisles. She had to remind herself that it couldn't possibly be the same girl whose skull she'd held in her hands two months before.

* * *

On 2 December 2011, police released the image to the media in an ambitious strategy to create public interest. There were thirty-five calls to police following the release of the facial approximation. Each tip was investigated but none led to the breakthrough police had been hoping for. It had been almost eighteen months since the bones had been found in the Belanglo State Forest and police still had no idea who the young woman was.

With no matches against missing persons records in Australia, and no one coming forward to identify Angel as their relative, police began to theorise that she must have been born elsewhere.

Despite taking on other homicide cases, Detective Attwood kept chipping away at the Belanglo investigation and further explored Interpol records in a bid to figure out Angel's true identity. But there were no women who matched Angel's profile overseas, either.

Dr Hayes watched out for developments and hoped her work might one day bring a family some answers. But months turned into years, and still Angel's identity remained a mystery.

'I really wanted to know who she was,' Dr Hayes recalled later. 'This young woman is somebody's child, somebody's friend, and she had the nation looking for her.'

Chapter 6

In winter, winds whip around the rickety corrugated-iron sheds and simple brick homes in Wynarka, stirring up the Murray Mallee's blush orange dirt. A rusty bell hanging outside the weatherboard post office sways with each gust.

The place would be deathly quiet if not for the roaring distant sound of road trains careering down the Karoonda Highway to and from Adelaide. Motorists crossing the border in and out of Victoria, 180 kilometres northeast, use the Karoonda Highway as a back road of sorts and an alternative to the National Highway A20 into Adelaide.

There isn't much to Wynarka, a blink-and-you'd-miss-it town in South Australia's sheep and grain farming region. Seventy-six permanent residents call the neat grid of residential streets home, but the town feels constantly empty. There'd be little reason to turn off the rural highway connecting the Murray River towns of Murray Bridge and Loxton in South Australia's south-eastern reaches. No petrol station. No toilet block. No fast food and no accommodation. People in Wynarka either live there, are visiting someone who lives there or have lost their way. It speaks to the Aboriginal meaning of the word Wynarka: 'a strayer'.

But in July 2015, word spread quickly about a discovery made 1.5 kilometres up the road on 14 July. Three men on their way to Adelaide had pulled over on the side of the Karoonda Highway just past Wynarka to answer nature's call.

The driver had pulled his car off the road onto an open patch of dirt between gum trees and an old truck tyre before wandering a little way off the road. There the westbound roadside was skirted by uneven ground, sandhills and thick scrub. A few metres from the road, where harsh scrub swallowed the pale rocky earth, the driver's gaze had drifted to a tattered suitcase lying on the ground, its contents spewed out on the dirt. He walked over to the scruffy bag. Grubby clothing — an old small pink jacket, black ballerina skirt and a tiny pair of silk shorts with the Holden car logo — was in a heap on the dry dirt.

Something else was visible in the sparse bush that afternoon that jarred. The man felt his back stiffen and his throat tighten as his eyes locked on to what looked like a jawbone among the pieces of clothing. Soon his two friends wandered over to see what he'd found.

The discovery was startling but the three men didn't call police immediately. However, disturbed by the haunting image, they made the call the next day, after they'd arrived in Adelaide. One of the men told the police operator he found what looked like part of a human skeleton; the bone was tiny as if it was from a child.

Within several hours the rural, desolate stretch of the Karoonda Highway was teeming with police. South Australia Police officers from a nearby town arrived first. Inside the faded, grubby, sixty-by-forty-centimetre suitcase, among the tattered clothing, was a small human skeleton, discarded in the most heinous of ways. Wrapped around the torso was a heavily stained elderberry towel; the tag read 'Down Under Towel'. A pathologist would later surmise that the stains on the towel and discoloured patches on the clothing were from blood. It was likely the remains were not in a skeletal state when they were stuffed into the suitcase and discarded like rubbish on the roadside.

While there was no skin or tissue on the bones, there was a mat of long blonde hair, and dull grey duct tape was wrapped around the skull, from the chin to just below the eye sockets. A baby's disposal nappy, soiled by the Murray Mallee dirt, was pressed against the side and front of the skull. When a forensic pathologist peeled back the tape, there was a blue and white dishcloth, similar to a Chux wipe, protruding from the top row of tiny teeth. Behind it was another cloth, scrunched in a ball towards the back of the jaw.

It was clear from the size of the bones that police were dealing with the remains of a child who had been subjected to an unspeakable death. The non-degradable strips of adhesive had maintained a grip over the tiny person's mouth and nose while the skin and tissue decomposed around it until a pile of bones was all that was left.

The Major Crime Investigation Branch, South Australia's specialist police unit that investigated homicides and sexual assaults, sent out a team of detectives from Adelaide. The area was locked down and a large blue tent placed over the remains while forensic officers began the grim task of examining the bones.

Like any crime scene examination, police started at the scene, ground zero, and worked outwards. Wynarka was the closest town to where the suitcase was found and detectives were tasked with making contact with every resident. They moved from house to house, asking people if they'd seen anything suspicious in recent days, weeks or months. The tone was cautious; investigators needed to be inquisitive not accusatory.

The residents of Wynarka were as shocked as anyone that a crime scene had turned up on their doorstep and they bent over backwards to help police. Their cooperation was welcomed, but it did throw up a few red herrings, including the sighting of a mysterious man who had been seen carrying a suitcase and walking along the Karoonda Highway in early 2015. There would be little reason for anyone to walk along the remote stretch of road; it was at least ten kilometres from Wynarka to the nearest town — Chapman Bore to the west or Karoonda to the east. There were few houses in between, just long empty stretches of countryside with stilted water tanks and quiet homesteads.

Two local women recalled seeing the man during an early morning walk. He hadn't offered them so much as a wave — odd behaviour in the Australian outback — and was carrying a dark-coloured suitcase. Public appeals for information about the mysterious man were pushed through the media but the man, along with a number of other suspicious sightings, were discounted.

Detectives would eventually door-knock residents across an area of 256 square kilometres, and talk to locals in eight different communities, from Tailem Bend to Murray Bridge and to Loxton in the north. There was also a sweeping letterbox drop through the Murray Mallee and stretching up to the Victorian border.

On 15 July, the bones were transported to the State Forensic Science Centre in Adelaide's CBD ahead of a post-

mortem examination the following day. The bones showed
no evidence of injury and the absence of soft tissue meant
a forensic pathologist couldn't definitively say whether the
young person suffered any other injuries before death.

Given the duct tape strangling the skull and the dishcloth
lodged in between the teeth, the pathologist reasoned the
cause of death could have been by asphyxiation.

Chapter 7

Detective Superintendent Des Bray squinted in the winter sun. It was seasonably cold in the Murray Mallee. The ground beneath his boots was still damp from the previous night's rains, and the reporters standing before him were wrapped in wool jackets.

He didn't envy the officers who'd been forced to spend the night on the side of the highway in the freezing cold as crime scene examiners. They worked under artificial light cast by towering floodlights, carefully picking apart every inch of scrub and earth surrounding the spot where the suitcase had been found.

It hadn't taken long for the media to figure out there was something major going on. One lane of the highway was completely closed and the road was lined with police cars, the red and blue flashing lights illuminating the trees along the dark stretch of road.

A flood of calls had been made to Crime Stoppers about the mysterious suitcase since the story hit the airwaves the day before. People had reported driving past the same spot in the weeks prior and noticing the suitcase. One person pulled over and dragged the suitcase closer to the road from out of the scrub; another was seen rifling through it but left it behind, probably assuming it contained just a bunch of ragged old clothes.

Roadworks had been carried out along the stretch of road as recently as late May 2015, and no one who worked on that job remembered finding or seeing a suitcase. It must have been dumped in the scrub a month, or at most six weeks, before it was found, police reasoned.

Detective Bray had travelled out to Wynarka from the Major Crime Investigation Branch hub in the CBD to address the steadily growing media pack observing the operation. After leading the Crime Gangs Task Force in South Australia for several years, Detective Bray had moved over to the Major Crime Investigations Branch in 2013. He had come in with fresh eyes and was unsettled by the number of unsolved murder cases on the books. Eventually he convinced senior management to give him more staff to tackle the backlog, and enacted a new practice where Major Crime would review every case over twelve months old in case any old evidence — fingerprints, DNA samples — could be processed with new technology. It became his legacy at the squad, and he emerged as the face behind solving many of South Australia's most chilling crimes.

In front of the camera, Detective Bray was calm, measured and empathetic. Off camera, to his friends and colleagues he was Doc, a bespectacled man with silver-white hair who could sit at a pub for hours exchanging war stories with colleagues. He was a seasoned storyteller who'd worked each end of the law-enforcement spectrum — from the cloak and dagger operations at the secretive Australian Crime Commission, to a beat cop in South Australia's suburbia.

Almost two weeks earlier, AFL Adelaide Crows coach Phil Walsh had been murdered and the investigation had fallen to Bray and his team. The death of the high-profile coach in a sports-mad city on 3 July had attracted nationwide attention, which had only just begun to subside when the Wynarka case landed on Bray's desk.

Before the milling media contingent, Detective Bray provided an update on the investigation. The information was scarce and there was no mention of the duct tape or the dishcloth found with the bones. It was a holdback strategy: those were details only the killer or someone involved in disposing of the child's body would know. Making the details public would give those responsible a plausible defence as to how they knew about the crucial information: *I read it in the newspaper or heard it mentioned on the news*. Keeping that information as tight as possible would be crucial to nailing a suspect down the track if they unwittingly mentioned duct tape or dishcloths to a third party or in an intercepted phone call.

'We can say that we believe the child died elsewhere,' Detective Bray explained. 'We also believe that the child was placed in a suitcase and brought to this location within about a month but the child had died sometime prior to that.'

There was one quote that hinted at the horror police had uncovered inside that suitcase: 'It is terribly clear that the child died a violent death under terrible circumstances … Everything about this case is tragic.'

There were no children of a similar age reported missing at the time in South Australia, and speculation was rife as to who the child in the suitcase might have been. Was it William Tyrell, the three-year-old boy dressed in a Spiderman suit who disappeared from his grandmother's backyard on the

New South Wales mid north coast in 2014? Or Madeleine McCann, the fair-haired toddler who vanished from her hotel bed in Portugal in 2007?

Both were far-fetched, and eventually ruled out when a forensic odontology assessment determined the child was a girl aged between 1.2 and 4.8 years, mid-point being three years, when she'd died as long ago as 2007. The fact that no one had come forward with this girl's name suggested no one knew she was missing and someone wanted to keep it that way.

Over the following weeks, detectives ended up with a list of names, potential victims, drawn from the databases of Commonwealth and state agencies, including Centrelink, and Crime Stoppers tip-offs.

If the child had been born in about 2005 or 2006, as police estimated, in 2015 she would have been nine or ten years old. Police checked the names of potential victims against school records to see if they were enrolled and whether they missed any follow-up immunisation appointments. There could be an innocent and reasonable explanation for it — the family might have moved overseas or the child died of natural causes.

The list contained the names of 175 children, some of which were from different states and territories. Names from interstate were collated, and a description of the young girl found in the suitcase — fair hair, ninety to ninety-five centimetres tall and Caucasian — was sent out to homicide squads in every state and territory. Detectives around the country were asked to check each name against enrolments at public, private and independent schools and to check whether there were any missing children matching the description that may have slipped through the cracks.

There wasn't. All 175 children on the list were eventually accounted for.

Police widened the criteria and were using sophisticated data analysis programs to come up with a new list of names. The same method was used — children born in the 2005–06 timeframe were cross-referenced against immunisation, schooling and welfare records.

When technology only got them so far, detectives began door-knocking relatives, friends and former partners, until they tracked down the whereabouts of a child. It was time-consuming and arduous police work, and a situation Detective Inspector Greg Hutchins, in charge of the team of twenty investigators working on the case, hadn't expected to find himself in. The second-in-charge to Detective Bray had spent thirty-seven years as a police officer. He had the patience of someone who had seen it all before and the composure of a hardened investigator who stopped being surprised a long time ago. Yet even he was unnerved that, a month after the suitcase's discovery, they still had no idea who the victim was. It seemed implausible in an age when everyone is connected, and movements are traced with smartphones and documented on social media. The girl in the suitcase seemed lost to society, stuck in a vacuum where government records didn't exist.

'In my thirty-seven years in police I have never had any job like it,' he said at the time. 'It is bizarre. Here we have a murder of a most vulnerable member of society. Someone would have celebrated her birth, bought or given her lovely clothes, had Christmas and Easter with her. It is so wrong to murder this little girl and so very wrong to dump her on the side of a road. It is bizarre in that it is highly likely she would be discovered and six weeks down the track we haven't identified her.'

It couldn't be ruled out that the girl had been living in a very dysfunctional environment on the fringe of society in an existence many would struggle to understand.

With the assistance of the Australian Centre for Ancient DNA, a DNA profile was extracted from the bones and uploaded to the national database. But there were no matches — unsurprising given the system did not match children with mothers.

For weeks, forensic officers pored over the bits of dirtied and ragged clothing found in the black Lanza-branded suitcase with the bones, looking for any traces of DNA on the heavily-soiled materials. There were thirty-odd items found in the bag: a black tutu with large multi-coloured spots on a tulle skirt; satin boxers; a single pink satin slipper with an embroidered butterfly; a purple T-shirt with the cartoon character Dora the Explorer; trackpants with the letters RA printed on the side, and a pink suede coat with fringing.

Some officers were tasked with flicking through hundreds of old junk mail leaflets, from stores like Big W and Target, trying to identify where the clothing came from.

At one press conference, a small mannequin was dressed in a blonde wig and a sparkly black tutu, the same as found in the suitcase. The tutu was one of twenty-eight sold at five Cotton On Kids stores, a popular Australian clothing outlet. Most of the other clothing was also mass-produced and had been sold at stores like Kmart and Big W.

A carefully hand-stitched quilt was the only item that appeared unique. The quilt's patches were octagonal and contained tiny pictures of animals, flowers and pumpkins. Black fabric with colourful musical notes bordered the blanket. While the 90-by-90-centimetre quilt had been machine-stitched, the pattern was complex and would have required the skills of an experienced quilter. Whether it was made specifically for this girl, police didn't know. It could have been made by a loving grandmother to keep the little girl warm, picked up second-hand at a charity store, or 'I would suggest, given the amount of work that goes into making one of those quilts, that someone loved that little girl and gave her that quilt,' Bray said at a press conference on 26 July, twelve days after the bones were found.

* * *

Over the following two months, police returned to Wynarka to search the roadside again and again. Mounted police started at opposite sides of the township, 15 kilometres out, and worked their way back towards the village in the hope their elevation would help spot evidence police on foot had missed.

More than 570 posters detailing the unsolved murder mystery were handed out to businesses across the region; 377 motorists were stopped and questioned at a police traffic stop; and 429 doors knocked on.

By early October, more than 1000 calls had been made to Crime Stoppers about the case — more than have been made for any other South Australia murder investigation in recent history.

Then, on the morning of 6 October, a woman who gave her name as Tanya Webber rang. 'It's a long shot but the girl in the suitcase could be Khandalyce Kiara Pearce,' Tanya told the operator. 'We haven't seen her in years. No one has seen her in a long time. Her mum is Karlie Jade Pearce-Stevenson.' Tanya explained she also recognised some of the clothing, particularly the pink coat and pants, and the hand-stitched quilt.

Two days later, on 8 October, Tanya rang again and politely pressed the importance of her information. She also had three photographs investigators needed to see, she said.

Logged as call No. 1267, Tanya's information was referred to South Australia detectives.

That night, Detective Sergeant Blake Horder, from the Major Crime Investigation Branch, called Tanya and asked her to email the photographs to him.

At 8:10 pm, under the subject line 'photos of Khandalyce', Tanya sent the following email:

Hi Blake,

Thank you for following up my concerns — these are the only photos that I have of Khandals (the pink dress she is wearing is the same as the photo I found on the web — attached).

I will see if I can find Colleen's (Khandal's grandmother) old USB stick that may have other photos.

Regards

Tanya Webber

Attached to the email were three very similar photos of a little girl about two years old. A black headband pushed her blonde hair off her face, and her tiny fingers were wrapped around the handles of a pram. She was wearing a dusty pink cotton dress with faint stripes. In one, she stared at the camera, her head slightly tilted.

Six minutes later, Detective Horder replied:

Thanks Tanya. Any information that we can get in this terrible case is much appreciated.

An hour later, Horder called Tanya and said that police had located Karlie interstate. However, in a follow-up email, he asked Tanya a series of detailed questions about the girls. Horder wanted to know where Khandalyce was born, what her mum Karlie's father's name was, if there was history of family illness, Karlie's last known mobile number, the name and contact details of Karlie's friend who started a Facebook page looking for her and the name of Karlie's grandmother who had hand-stitched the quilt.

The following morning, Tanya's response came through. She was able to answer all Horder's questions and asked whether Karlie had been located. Tanya was an old friend of Karlie's stepfather, Scott, who she'd met in Alice Springs in the early 2000s when Scott was married to Karlie's mother, Colleen Margaret Povey.

An hour later, Horder called Tanya to explain there had been a mistake. The Karlie police had located was *not* Karlie Jade Pearce-Stevenson, but another woman with a similar name.

Tanya emailed Horder a few hours later with the mobile phone number of Karlie's best friend and information about Karlie's mother's last-known contact with her daughter.

> Just a thought; when Colleen last heard from her in 2011 she transferred money from her TIO bank account into Karlie's bank account to help her get 'home' (back to Alice Springs) — hoping this might be another way to locate where she was the time she withdrew the money?
>   Thanks Tanya.

On 11 October, Karlie's stepfather, Scott Povey, emailed a photograph of Khandalyce's blanket to Horder. The photograph showed Khandalyce sitting in a stroller with a hand-stitched quilt that Scott's mother had made for the little girl in 2007.

In the photograph, Khandalyce, with grey-blue eyes and sandy blonde hair, looked no more than twelve months old. She was dressed in a bright red T-shirt and clutched a colourful Rubik's cube in her right hand. The top third of the photo showed the multi-coloured musical notes that made up the quilt's distinctive edges.

Scott pointed out the similarities between the quilt in the photo and the quilt found in the suitcase. The resemblance had sent 'shivers down his spine', he said.

Khandalyce Kiara Pearce became the strongest line of inquiry Task Force Mallee detectives had received. Now the investigation took off at a rapid pace after countless dead-ends and gruelling groundwork.

Police discovered that Khandalyce, who would be aged nine by now, had been immunised when she was eighteen months old but had never been enrolled in a school in any state or territory in Australia. Instead, it seemed, from late 2008 the little girl had disappeared.

Detectives requested access to a record of Khandalyce's newborn screening test, the Guthrie Card, taken at Alice Springs Hospital. Since the late 1960s babies have undergone pinprick tests in maternity wards in Australia two or three days after birth, and the blood sample is used to test for a range of congenital diseases. The blood is blotted onto a piece of card, and the length of time these cards — essentially containing a person's DNA — are kept by health departments differs across states and territories.

Newborn blood samples taken in the Northern Territory are generally stored in Adelaide or Brisbane. The laws of the respective states dictate forensic access. Khandalyce's Guthrie Card was stored at the Women's and Children's Hospital in North Adelaide.

At the request of South Australia Police, forensic biologists generated a DNA profile from the blood sample and compared it against the DNA profile from the bones found in the suitcase. It matched. After three months of searching, police had put a name and a face to the little girl in the suitcase.

On the morning of 12 October, two Major Crime detectives called Scott and informed him they had confirmed that the remains found in the suitcase were in fact Khandalyce's.

The detectives requested that Scott and his family stay quiet about the development. They couldn't afford the information getting out at this stage, as it would tip off those involved in Khandalyce's death. The focus would now shift to finding out who had been responsible for putting the vulnerable two-year-old there in the first place, and they needed to gain as much ground as they could without the risk of interference.

Already crippled with grief, Scott was faced with what felt like an impossible task. Still, for nine days he and his family cut themselves off from the world they knew, ignoring phone calls and risking friendships to keep the secret.

All the while, they were tortured by the obvious question: if Khandalyce was dead, where was Karlie?

Chapter 8

I t had been five years since forensic biologist Kara Wilson had extracted a DNA profile from a small piece of bone found in the Belanglo State Forest. The profile had been sitting in the national database, waiting to be matched to another case and to provide police with answers.

Wilson had worked on hundreds of other forensic cases since, carefully retrieving traces of DNA from torn clothing found at crime scenes or bones uncovered in desolate locations. Sadly, it wasn't unusual for the lab to receive cases involving long-term unidentified remains like Angel.

Police referred thirty-three missing persons cases to Wilson, hopeful for a match with the bones found in the forest. But each time she would have to call Detective Attwood with bad news.

'We were both feeling the frustration when we had to exclude somebody,' Wilson later recalled. 'But we were ticking another box, really, to keep chipping away at it.'

Then, on 15 October 2015, Ms Wilson received a call from the Forensic Intelligence and Results Management (FIRM) unit that made her drop what she was doing. A DNA profile would be sent via email shortly. It related to a little girl found in a suitcase in rural South Australia a few months prior.

After using Khandalyce's medical records to identify the bones found in the suitcase, the focus had turned to her mother. If the toddler was dead, where was Karlie?

After the Crime Stoppers call, South Australia detectives had pored over missing persons and unidentified remains records looking for cases of young women who would fit Karlie's profile. Even before Khandalyce was identified, they'd noted the case of Angel, and the timeframe and age bracket fitted.

Karlie had left Alice Springs in late 2008 and travelled down to Adelaide; she'd met a friend at a shopping centre in Adelaide in November that year, before she went to Canberra for a while. Canberra was less than two hours' drive from Belanglo State Forest and Karlie's age would fall within the approximate age range of Angel.

South Australia Police contacted the on-call team at the NSW Homicide Squad and filled them in on the state of the investigation. The information needed to be kept confidential — they wanted to compare Khandalyce's DNA profile against the bones found in Belanglo State Forest in 2010.

To some officers privy to the request, the suggestion bordered on the unbelievable. The bodies were found five years apart in different states; the idea that the victims could be mother and child was hard to fathom.

Plus Karlie didn't fit Angel's profile. Based on the stable isotope testing, Angel was probably someone who spent a lot of time overseas, not a young woman born and bred in Australia.

Given his history with the Angel case, Detective Attwood was brought into the fold. The prospect that Angel might finally be identified was undeniably exciting. But privately, according to colleagues, he initially had his doubts there could be a link.

After years of mismatches, Kara Wilson shared some of Attwood's scepticism. She'd heard about the little girl in the suitcase in South Australia and was aware police hadn't been able to identify the child, despite releasing photographs of clothing and a blanket found with the remains. It was not dissimilar to the frustrations encountered in the Angel case in New South Wales.

Wilson was usually unmoved when she received requests for DNA comparison against Angel, but there was something in the FIRM staffer's voice that suggested this was out of the ordinary. 'They're excited about this one,' the staff member told her.

South Australia Police wanted to know if the little girl found in the suitcase could be the biological daughter of the woman found in Belanglo.

When the email arrived Wilson printed off two pages of paper, one with the DNA profile of the bones found in Belanglo and the other the profile of Khandalyce.

A child inherits half of her DNA from her mother and half from her father. A biological child's profile therefore will match half of the parent's profile it is being compared against. Wilson placed the pages on the desk in front of her and looked to see whether the DNA profiles from Khandalyce and the bones found in Belanglo shared a type, or allele, at each of the locations tested. A person inherits one allele from each of their parents.

The two profiles are then entered into a statistical calculation to determine the strength of the result. Two people might share alleles by chance because those alleles are more common in the population generally, and the calculation would produce a lower value to reflect that. But if less-common alleles are shared by a parent and child, the calculation would show a higher probability that the two people were related.

To make the comparison, Wilson looked to match allele at twenty different locations. Almost immediately her trained eye did just that.

As the reality of what she was seeing dawned on her, she could barely contain her excitement. She'd compared thousands of DNA profiles throughout her career but she still couldn't believe what she was seeing.

Oh, my God, she thought, checking the comparison again and again, just in case she'd missed something. A job that usually took a few minutes took twenty-five minutes, as Wilson made sure there was no room for error.

'You really need to look at this now,' Wilson said to her superior, Dr Bruce. 'We're looking at a paternity comparison, so we need to know if these two profiles could be biologically related, mother and daughter. Can you have a look now? It's really important.'

Bruce turned his attention to the papers as Wilson hovered behind him, frozen in anticipation.

'Yes, indeed, this DNA profile could be from the biological child of that individual,' he soon confirmed.

'Do you know what case this is?' asked an incredulous Wilson. 'It's the woman found in Belanglo State Forest in 2010. Remember the unidentified remains found by the dirt bike riders? South Australia Police sent up a DNA profile this morning from a child found in a suitcase back in July. It's highly likely they're mother and daughter.'

After five years delivering bad news to Detective Attwood, Wilson was finally going to be able to tell him something positive.

She grabbed her phone. 'Tim, its Kara Wilson from FASS. I've just compared the profile South Australia Police sent through with Angel's bones. It looks like they are mother and daughter,' she said.

'Yessss,' Attwood replied.

'I think he had a strong inkling this would pan out, that was my feeling, that police were basically waiting for us to confirm,' Ms Wilson reflected years later.

Detective Attwood stressed the importance of keeping the breakthrough under wraps. 'It's a great result, but we're working really hard on this and need to keep it quiet.'

He didn't have to tell Ms Wilson twice; she understood unequivocally. There had been five years of trial and error to that point and she wasn't about to jeopardise the case, no matter how thrilled she was.

The next day, South Australia Police sent Kara Wilson a reference DNA sample drawn from medical records in the Northern Territory, belonging to Karlie Pearce-Stevenson. They wanted confirmation that Karlie was indeed the woman whose bones had been found in Belanglo State Forest five years prior, and the mother of Khandalyce.

Still elated from the previous day's breakthrough, Wilson carefully compared the DNA profiles. She took a deep breath as she turned to Dr Bruce with a look of shock on her face for the second time in less than a day. The DNA profiles matched.

Only a handful of investigators at the NSW Homicide Squad were briefed on the breakthrough; even their colleagues weren't allowed to know what was going on.

Detective Superintendent Mick Willing was the commander of the squad at the time and remembered receiving Detective Attwood's phone call on 16 October 2015.

Willing recalled that Detective Attwood revealed he was shaking. 'Boss, it's her,' he said.

Part II

Disappearance

Part 1

Disappearance

Chapter 9

As a child, she was occasionally dubbed 'Mouse', due to her tiny frame, but Karlie never liked it. She may have been little, but she was vivacious and adventurous, and made the most of growing up in the Australian outback. Even though she was barely tall enough to see over the dashboard, she loved going on long trips with her stepdad in his road train, camping in the desert and fishing in the northern reaches of Spencer Gulf.

Born on 7 August 1988 in Alice Springs Hospital, Karlie Jade Pearce-Stevenson was her mum, Colleen's, first child. Karlie had her mother's eyes and her mother's stubbornness, and they were close from the start, evident to everyone by the way Karlie constantly hovered around Colleen's legs. Colleen Stevenson, who was known to friends and family as Col, had left Karlie's father, Bruce Pearce, while she was pregnant with Karlie, moving from South Australia to Alice Springs in central Australia to live with her sister, Raylene Bell, and to be near her other sister, Sharon. Less than half the size of Darwin, the Northern Territory capital 1500 kilometres to the north, Alice Springs has a population of just over 25,000, and while it has the buzz of a tourist destination, it has the close-knit community of an isolated outback town.

Ray and Colleen were joined at the hip and shared a house until Karlie was a few months shy of two years old, when Colleen met Scott Povey. Scott was from the Adelaide Hills and had made a stopover in Alice on his way north on the famous Ghan, the iconic red passenger train that travelled through the heart of Australia from Adelaide to Darwin via Alice Springs.

His plan had been to eventually get to Darwin but Scott, a truck driver with piercing blue eyes, took up an offer of work in Alice. When he met Colleen he stayed, and a couple of years later, in 1992, Karlie's brother, Luke, was born.

Colleen and Scott were married in a park outside the Alice Springs Courthouse on 4 February 1995. By then, the family of four were living in a house in Braitling, just around the corner from Colleen's sisters, her mum, Connie, and friends.

Colleen and her sisters, Ray and Sharon, babysat each other's children at a moment's notice, and the cousins spent weekends splashing in Aunty Ray's pool. When Karlie was growing up, the aunties and cousins would play netball together each Saturday at the local courts on Undoolya Road.

The Povey family home, at the end of a quiet cul de sac behind a green fence, was always impeccably neat; Colleen's sisters often joked that it resembled a model home because nothing was ever out of place. Nothing except Karlie's room, where piles of toys and clothes were strategically hidden under blankets so her parents wouldn't notice. On one occasion, fed up with the mess, Scott stormed into Karlie's room and, demanding she clean up her act, he began to throw her things out the bedroom window. She ran outside and began throwing them back in again. Soon they were both laughing. It was an insight into a complex relationship that could be tense at times. But there was fun, too, and as well as camping and exploring, Scott and Karlie would often spend mornings drinking coffee together on the back patio or would head out to the speedway with friends on weekends.

But, like many fathers, Scott was the disciplinarian in the household, and he had rules he expected his children to follow. As Karlie entered her teenage years, she began to push against those rules, a rebellious rite of passage for many girls that age. When Karlie was in Year 10 at Alice Springs High School, her teacher called Scott to tell him his stepdaughter had been skipping school. It was the latest in a string of disobedient behaviour. Karlie had also been caught lying about stealing smokes from her mum and change from her wallet. It felt like nothing her parents said or did made a difference.

Then one school day, Scott walked into Karlie's bedroom to find her reading a magazine on the bed, dressed in her school uniform. He shouted at her and in a split second, Scott raised his hand and slapped her on the back of the legs.

He'd never laid a hand on his children before, he said later, and it shocked him as much as it did Karlie, who bolted out of the house in tears. Instantly, Scott regretted the punishment. He'd thought it might put the fear of god into her but he was left feeling sick to his stomach. 'What I did was wrong and I've ripped myself to pieces ever since,' he would later recall.

Karlie ran to her aunt's house in tears but eventually returned home. She forgave her stepdad, but their relationship continued to be a challenge — when Scott pushed, Karlie pulled.

In Year 10, Karlie left school and decided to move in with her grandmother, Connie. Connie was the rock of the family, a matriarch who looked after her grandchildren whenever required, especially when they were young and their mothers were doing shift work at a local service station.

Connie's home had been a respite for not only young family members, but friends too. Her relatives suspect her hospitality came back to bite her in 2010 when she was charged with cannabis possession. They claim a man staying with her at the time had supplied the eighty-year-old grandmother marijuana to ease the pain of an ongoing ankle injury.

Another of Karlie's rocks during her teenage years was a young woman called Tanya Webber. Tanya worked with Colleen at a stationery shop in Alice, and despite their age difference —Tanya was ten years younger than Colleen — they became best friends. It was a bond that extended to Karlie, and Tanya became the teenager's close confidante as she navigated adolescence. Karlie would often visit Tanya and, as she got older, minded her house, dog and cat when Tanya was away on work trips.

Karlie began to pick up shifts at Aunty Ray's snack bar and soon was begging to be allowed to work behind the till while her cousins stocked the fridge. Despite her troubles at home, Karlie seemed to enjoy the responsibility that came with handling the takings and she never took a cent. The most strife she got herself in was when Ray found her smoking cigarettes in the staff toilet.

Karlie had always displayed a nurturing fascination with parenthood and children. As a small girl she'd doted over her little brother and when her baby cousins were born she loved to hold them. She often spoke to her family about how she'd bring up her own child one day and the sort of life she wanted for them.

Then, at age seventeen, while she was still living at Connie's, Karlie found out she was pregnant. According to her family, the pregnancy was a result of a casual hook-up with a friend who wasn't up for playing the role of a father.

It didn't matter to Karlie. She was thrilled by the prospect of having a child and was prepared for life as a single mother. However, she was apprehensive about telling her stepfather. But when Scott saw the grin on her face, he couldn't be angry.

In June 2006, Khandalyce Kiara Pearce was born. Khandalyce, or Khandals, as the family came to call her, had her mother's almond eyes, blonde hair, charisma and endearing cheekiness.

Colleen and Scott were thrilled to have a granddaughter and Khandals was welcomed into the extended family. For Khandals' first birthday, Scott's mother gave her stepgranddaughter a unique quilt she had made using colours and patterns chosen with the little girl in mind.

Unwilling to let Karlie lose sight of the responsibility that came with being a parent, Connie, who'd raised her own three daughters to be strong and assertive women, was supportive but firm while Karlie lived under her roof.

Connie agreed to look after Khandalyce when Karlie went out with her friends at night, mindful of the fact her granddaughter was still a teenager.

But when the baby started crying in the early hours of the morning, it was Karlie's responsibility to feed her — hangover or no hangover. 'You're her mother, you have to get up and look after her,' Connie would remind Karlie as she stumbled, bleary-eyed, to the kitchen.

Karlie had a couple of short-term relationships as a teenager, but in late 2006 she met Robbie Frampton, who would become her most serious boyfriend to date. Karlie had caught Robbie's eye at Alice night spot Malanka party bar, where he worked on the door as a security guard. Later they met through a mutual friend at a shopping centre in Alice Springs.

Soon Robbie was staying over at Connie's, but after months crammed into Connie's spare bedroom, Karlie and Robbie were looking for a place of their own.

But money was tight; Karlie was caring for Khandalyce full-time and Robbie was working as a delivery driver for Prime Cut Meat Supplies in Alice Springs. Then Scott had an idea. He had a mate who was president of the Alice Springs Speedway committee, and there was an apartment on the property usually reserved for a caretaker. If Karlie and Robbie were willing to look after the place and give it a lick of paint, it was theirs for $100 a week rent.

The young couple jumped at the offer, and within a few weeks they'd settled into the tiny apartment, now decked out with donated furniture. It was a relief to have a place of their own — somewhere to share after almost a year of dating. Karlie's life appeared to settle; she had a boyfriend her family approved of and her relationship with Scott, who'd often pop over to the speedway for a beer, was amicable.

Robbie became the person he believed Karlie was after; he loved her unconditionally and treated Khandalyce as if she was his own. But he also knew that Karlie dreamt of getting away from her tight-knit hometown, where everyone knew everyone's business and gossip was a sport. Already he could see that she wanted more than Alice Springs had to offer.

Chapter 10

In late 2007, Robbie was at work at Prime Cut Meat Supplies when a man he recognised from a car yard down the road walked in and introduced himself. The man said his name was Daniel Marshall and he was relatively new to town. Did Robbie know of anyone who smoked marijuana, he asked.

Daniel had been sourcing drugs from a warehouse in Adelaide, driving the haul back to Alice Springs and selling it for an impressive profit. His customer base wasn't bad but he could see there was more money to be made.

The two men became friendly, and Robbie came to learn that Daniel had spent the past several months travelling around Australia in a caravan with his partner, Hazel, his step-kids, Willow and Ryan, and daughter Lauryn. They'd settled in Alice Springs in search of work.

When they first came to town, they'd stayed at the Stuart Park Caravan and Cabin Tourist Park across the road from Araluen Park. Daniel had picked up work at a used car yard and a mechanic's workshop until he'd earned enough income for the family to upgrade from the caravan park to a two-bedroom apartment and finally a townhouse.

Daniel appeared to have taken on the role of father to Willow, Ryan and Lauryn, but Robbie felt that he didn't treat Hazel with as much care. Nevertheless, eventually Robbie started taking Karlie and Khandalyce with him when he went to visit Daniel at home. Khandals and Lauryn were about the same age and they'd play together in the backyard. When Karlie and Robbie's bathroom was being renovated, Karlie would shower at Hazel and Daniel's house, and afternoons were spent in the backyard as their daughters played.

A couple of times a month Daniel would take off to Adelaide on a drug run and return with a haul of cannabis to sell around Alice Springs. He was usually discreet with his earnings but occasionally he'd proudly lay out the fifty dollar notes on the kitchen bench in front of Robbie and Karlie.

And then there were the drugs. While Hazel only smoked marijuana, Daniel was into the hard stuff — ecstasy and speed. It was a world Karlie had never explored but as she came to associate with Daniel and Hazel more and more in mid to late 2008, she began to pick up their habits.

It is with the benefit of hindsight that Robbie can say he had a feeling something was developing between Daniel and Karlie. Years later, as he reflected on the signs of deceit, he still chose his words carefully, reluctant to speak ill of the girl he loved.

He remembered in 2008 turning up unannounced at home, in between deliveries for work, and finding Daniel's car parked in the driveway.

There were also text messages on Karlie's phone from Daniel, thanking her for a 'great time', about which Robbie had no idea.

However, despite his niggling suspicions, Robbie chose to believe that Karlie wouldn't go behind his back and kept quiet.

According to Robbie, it was around this time that Karlie, influenced heavily by Daniel, moved from smoking cannabis to using methamphetamines, commonly known as ice.

On 16 September 2008, Robbie woke to an alarming text message from Daniel on his phone. Daniel said he'd been in a bad car accident and needed Robbie to come to Alice Springs Hospital.

In the hospital emergency department, Robbie found Daniel inconsolable. Apparently, Daniel had been driving in the middle of the night from Alice Springs to Adelaide when he'd swerved to avoid a kangaroo and had lost control of the car.

Willow and Ryan, who had been in the back seat, were dead and Hazel, who had to be airlifted to the Royal Adelaide Hospital, was in a bad way. Like Daniel, Lauryn had survived with minor injuries.

Over the following weeks, Daniel travelled between Alice Springs and Adelaide to see Hazel in hospital, and Robbie watched as his drug use spiralled out of control.

Around the same time, Robbie felt Karlie growing more distant and their relationship began to buckle. Then, in late October 2008, they had an argument that ended in Karlie telling her boyfriend she wanted to leave him.

When Robbie returned home from work later that day he found their apartment empty. A note from Karlie informed him their relationship was over.

While the warning signs had been there, Robbie felt blindsided; he'd figured they loved each other enough to get through whatever issues they had.

He raced around to Connie's house in search of Karlie but she wasn't there. Then he went to Scott and Colleen's place but Karlie wasn't there either.

Finally, he spotted Karlie's car at a friend's house in town. On the windscreen of the maroon-coloured 1996 Holden Commodore station wagon that Scott and Colleen had given Karlie, Robbie left a heartfelt letter.

He never got a response.

* * *

Karlie returned to stay at Connie's house.

Her family were as perplexed as Robbie as to why she'd left him. He seemed like a nice, decent bloke and someone who genuinely cared for Karlie and Khandals.

One night, as they sat around Connie's dining table, Ray asked Karlie what had happened.

'I just don't love him anymore,' Karlie said with a shrug of her shoulders.

The family were also worried about the change in Karlie's physical appearance. She'd always been naturally small and slender; when she was little, her mum and aunties would tie her underwear in a knot to ensure it stayed on her tiny hips while she ran around playing.

But towards the end of 2008, Karlie's slight frame alarmed even those closest to her.

'Are you on drugs?' an unapologetic Ray asked once.

Karlie had scoffed at the idea, but tried to put her aunt's mind at ease. 'No, Aunty Ray,' she replied with a subtle eye roll. 'I smoke a joint every now and again but that's it.'

'I'm not talking about that,' Ray pressed. 'You're so skinny. You've lost so much weight.'

The concern seemed lost on Karlie, who light-heartedly assured Ray there was nothing to worry about. 'I promise, Aunty Ray, I've always looked like this,' she said.

Subtle changes in Karlie's behaviour were also fuelling her family's suspicions about her drug abuse. One day she'd be her normal, happy self and the next she'd be moody and agitated.

Once, at Colleen and Scott's, a cup of coffee had fallen from Karlie's shaking hands and she'd glanced at her stepdad sheepishly. Her pupils had been as big as saucepans, Scott recalled.

In November 2008, Karlie dropped by Colleen's workplace, Territory Surgical Supplies, to see her mother and to use her work computer.

A post on social media hinted at her buoyant mood. Karlie Stevenson 'is being very bored trying to work this all out.! Xoxoxo', the Facebook post read in a reference to trying to navigate the new social media platform.

Colleen wasn't in her office when Karlie visited that day, but she returned to her desk to find a bunch of flowers and a note: 'To Mum, love KJ xo'.

A day or two later, Karlie and Khandalyce dropped by Colleen and Scott's home with a man whom Karlie introduced as Daniel.

Colleen Povey immediately felt uneasy about the stranger. He didn't seem to be her daughter's type but it was difficult to tell whether they were just friends or something more. Collen hoped it was the former.

As she talked to her daughter, Colleen couldn't take her eyes off the tall, brooding man. The deep lines etched in his forehead made him appear older than his thirty-four years. He avoided eye contact and muttered only a few words; it seemed like he wanted to get the pleasantries over and done with as quickly as possible.

Tanya arrived. The man took two steps up to the patio, shook her hand without looking her in the eye, then retreated again. As the three women chatted, he stood by himself watching Khandalyce, dressed in a pair of silk boxer shorts in the sweltering Northern Territory heat, run around the backyard with a toy pram. The little girl was just like her mother had been as a child; energetic, happy and fascinated by anything to do with babies.

When the man yelled at Khandalyce for running around the entertainment area, it didn't sit well with Colleen, and she had to bite her tongue. This bloke barely knew the family; who was he to be dishing out fatherly discipline? Colleen expected Karlie to pull him up on his behaviour, but Karlie didn't react.

Karlie had other things on her mind, and she announced that she was going on a trip to Adelaide with the man and Khandalyce the following day.

In fact, it would be the second trip Karlie was to make to South Australia in a month. She'd gone south with Daniel in late October, a few days after breaking up with Robbie. But Colleen and Tanya knew nothing about that trip.

According to Scott, Colleen sensed that something wasn't right and asked Karlie to leave Khandalyce with her this time. While Colleen trusted her twenty-year-old daughter to make the best decisions for Khandals, there was something unsettling about this man that made her insist on keeping the toddler in Alice Springs.

But Karlie refused to leave without her daughter and Colleen had no other choice but to accept her decision.

Dressed in a camouflage skirt, a white cotton halter top and a red jacket, Karlie smoked in silence, sharing an ashtray with Colleen and Tanya. She seemed sullen and stressed, like something was on her mind. No longer was she the giggling, sociable young woman her family knew and loved.

Soon it was time for them to leave. As Karlie walked out the front door of her family home that day, she stopped to hug her mum and Tanya goodbye.

Years later, Tanya would recall wrapping her arms around Karlie and Khandalyce and wishing them safe travels to South Australia.

The stranger, still skittish and avoiding eye contact, followed the girls out the door towards Karlie's car, which was parked in the driveway.

Tanya stopped him. 'Look after them,' she said.

***

In November 2008, a day or two after they said goodbye to Colleen and Tanya, Karlie, Khandalyce and Daniel had made it to Port Augusta, a railway junction town in South Australia at the top of the Eyre Peninsula. Karlie's father, Bruce Pearce, was based there but wasn't home to welcome her; he was in Western Australia working in the mines. It was a shame because he was desperate to meet his granddaughter, Khandalyce. He wanted to take her fishing down at the shacks, a row of fibro and weatherboard holiday homes at Commissariat Point on the western side of the gulf, just south of Port Augusta. There he planned to show Khandalyce how to throw pots out for crabs and catch whiting, just as he'd done with her mother when she'd visited him on weekends as a kid.

Bruce had seen less of Karlie in her teenage years, but she'd stayed in touch via regular phone calls. Sometimes she'd ask him for a loan to pay for bond or rent. Bruce knew he'd never see the cash again but he obliged. Rather than deposit the money directly into Karlie's account, he'd ask for the realtor's bank account details. It seemed like an overbearing condition but, in Bruce's eyes, he was teaching Karlie the value of money and wanted to make sure it went to the right place.

Fortunately, Bruce's mum, Lorna, was home, and Karlie and Khandalyce called in on her to stay a night or two. When they arrived Lorna had immediately scooped up Khandalyce and showered her with affection.

'I love you, Nanny,' Khandalyce said.

A decade later, Lorna could still remember the sweet sound of Khandalyce's voice.

'I was so happy to have them staying at my house, it gave me more time with them,' Lorna recalled. 'I feel like I loved them to death when they arrived. Both girls were very happy to see me and were carefree. But then he turned up and the mood changed.'

The person Lorna referred to as 'he' was Daniel, Karlie's new friend. Karlie introduced Daniel to her grandmother and instantly Lorna was unimpressed by the man's lack of eye contact and evasive manner. Every question she asked was met with a one-word answer and there was no effort made to engage with Lorna. Karlie's grandmother felt ignored, and decided from that moment on she disliked the man. There was something unsettling about his presence. Perhaps she could sense the irrepressible drug use that put him constantly on edge and made him agitated.

Karlie's aunt Alison was there too, and she noticed the dynamic between Daniel and Karlie. She wanted to know if her niece was comfortable with this strange man and the sudden move interstate.

'I'm really happy and everything's good. You don't need to worry,' Karlie reassured her.

Later, Karlie took Khandalyce into the bathroom to give her a bath. Afterwards, the toddler reappeared smelling of soap and with a towel draped around her little shoulders. Karlie wrapped her arms around her daughter lovingly and rubbed the towel gently to dry off Khandals' soft skin.

Spotting Alison holding a camera, Karlie lifted her chin slightly, pulled Khandalyce in a little closer and smiled.

Alison took the snap. It was one of the last photos ever taken of the mother and daughter.

Chapter 11

Daniel Marshall, the man with whom Karlie was travelling in November 2008, was in fact Daniel Holdom, the only son of Clara and her first husband, Glen Holdom. Clara and Glen had both grown up in farming families and had fallen in love when Clara was fifteen. Clara had gravitated towards Glen, a brooding man of five foot eight with dark hair and eyes, and liked the idea of building a life with him. The couple were together for two years before they married, a union that turned out to be an utter disappointment to Clara. She found her husband 'very spoilt and demanding', their relationship isolating and devastatingly lonely.

Clara gave birth to their first child in 1970, but four years later, when she found out she was pregnant again, Glen wasn't happy. Years later she would tell a social worker that Glen — whose drinking and long absences from home perpetuated her unhappiness — wanted her to have an abortion.

Clara was resolute, believing another baby might in fact save her troubled marriage. She gave birth to Daniel James Holdom on 7 October 1974. Daniel was the spitting image of his father, but came into the world unwanted, bruised and screaming, following a traumatic birth that left him unresponsive. Even Clara admitted the first sight of her son — black and blue from the use of forceps during labour — scared her. It only increased a niggling paranoia in her mind that something bad was going to happen to him, that something dark was born the day he came in to the world. In the years before he was born, Clara's mother and brother had died in separate circumstances and, foggy with grief, Clara feared Daniel would meet the same fate. She met the newborn's basic needs but never formed the bond a mother was meant to have with her baby. She deliberately kept her distance from him and withheld love and affection.

As a baby, Daniel screamed throughout the night and refused to be settled, which only fuelled Clara's fears. One sleep-deprived night she reached into his cot, placed her hands over his small shoulders and shook him violently. She told the social worker she managed to stop herself before inflicting any irreparable damage.

When Daniel was about fourteen months old, Clara's marriage to Glen finally self-destructed and she kicked him out of the family home. To support her two children she worked on a dairy farm, where she fell in love with her boss.

When Daniel was just shy of two years old, Clara and her new partner relocated to Orange in New South Wales, a country town west of the Great Dividing Range, surrounded by rolling farmland and open plains. Daniel grew up in a housing commission home, rented for seventy-five dollars a week, with his three stepbrothers and another relative. However, according to records later tendered in court, Clara's partner saw Daniel as his rival, a competitor for her affection, and was abusive towards the boy. The man claimed his treatment of Daniel was justified because the boy was not a 'good child', historical child welfare documents state.

In admissions to social workers and psychiatrists later tendered in court, Daniel Holdom claimed physical and emotional abuse at the hands of his stepfather between the ages of three or four and nine was relentless.

At primary school, Daniel's uniform was crumpled and unwashed, his black hair shaggy and unkempt. 'We knew that he was a loner,' a former schoolmate who went to Orange Public School remembered years later. 'We knew there were problems at home for him. I don't think any of us really knew him at school because he was a recluse.'

Daniel was regularly seen sitting outside the principal's office because he'd raided bins around the school or rifled through students' lunchboxes looking for food. Girls steered clear of him because they found him unsettling; and boys found him odd. He was a peculiar young boy who never quite fitted in.

Daniel's practice of lying and thieving was evident from a young age. He would steal money from his mother's wallet to buy sweets at the shop with one of his stepbrothers, and pinch cash from the lunch orders at school. According to records later tendered in court, the Department of Community Services (DOCS) intervened when he was eight years old and placed him in temporary foster care. As a result, Holdom held a long grudge against his mother, who he felt had chosen his stepfather over him.

In 1984, Clara intervened. Daniel, then nine years old, had been placed back in the care of his family on 17 May 1984 after a period in temporary foster care. According to case notes from the time that were later tendered in court, Clara — hands shaking and eyes bloodshot from crying —

discreetly approached a DOCS caseworker at Orange Local Court. Her husband had beaten Daniel after he ran away from school and she was afraid of what would happen if they returned home.

Clara and the five children caught a train to Sydney and stayed at a women's refuge in the city's west. The family eventually reunited and Clara went with her partner to DOCS and said they couldn't handle Daniel; he was stealing and running away from school constantly. They needed him out of their house.

Between the ages of eight and fifteen, Daniel bounced between his biological father, his grandparents and six foster homes. He attended several different schools, two of which he later said he was expelled from, and his behaviour — from ripping fur off a cat to hoarding food in his room — tested the patience of even the most experienced foster carers.

'Danny has an extremely low self-esteem and is very uncoordinated physically, and is the type of child who tends to irritate most care givers,' a caseworker remarked in court documents dated August 1984. 'He is extremely attention-seeking and accident-prone, and will require an exceptional situation if he is to resolve his problems and to have any chance of leading a fulfilled life.'

The caseworker couldn't find a foster home, so at the age of nine, Daniel was sent to live with his father, Glen, on a property in Moorland, north of Taree. There he discovered what it was like to form a close bond with a parent. Glen and his new partner had been unable to have children of their own and, according to DOCS case notes, quickly jumped at the chance to take Daniel out of the toxic environment he was in. The boy was enrolled in Moorland Public School and his attendance was well above what it had been, his behaviour in the classroom was sound, and he made friends. Life under his father's roof was stable.

That same year, Orange Children's Court committed Daniel into Glen's care until he was sixteen years old. But in 1985, Glen landed work driving trucks near Tamworth, and Daniel was sent to live with his grandparents in Johns River. There he was enrolled in a new school, where his excellent performance as a student initially continued. But within a few months there had been a shift; with Glen away, Daniel no longer wanted to live in the Taree area and he began to act out. He spoke of moving back to Orange to a boys' home or to be with his mother.

DOCS was reluctant to send him back and looked to relatives for help. An aunt lived on a dairy farm with her husband, and while they had no kids, they worked long hours and wouldn't have time to care for a child. Glen was in such deep financial stress that he had to continue working; he didn't have the means or time to look after his son anymore. Daniel lived with his grandparents for several months but his behaviour started to deteriorate again, to the point they could no longer deal with his tantrums, screaming and belligerence.

He was moved into residential care with the United Protestant Association in Orange. On weekends once or twice a month he visited his mother and stepbrothers, times he looked forward to. However, Clara would regularly cancel the visits because, while she'd broken up Daniel's stepfather, he often returned home unannounced.

In 1986, an apprehended domestic violence order was granted to protect Clara and Daniel from Clara's former partner.

At school, Daniel was excelling and his behaviour had turned around; tantrums were few and far between and while he struggled to concentrate in class, he was well liked. At Canobolas High School he was receiving regular merit awards, competing in swimming carnivals, playing soccer or ten pin bowling on the weekends and was an enthusiastic member of the Boys' Brigade.

Daniel's version is that he was kicked out of school at fifteen — historical records place him at high school until Year 9. However, it is unclear whether he was expelled or chose to leave school, given a mid-year report from his principal in Year 8 labelled him a 'very co-operative student who always tries to please'. One way or another, he finished school then moved out of home and landed a job at a milk factory.

Growing up, Daniel had dreamt of being a chef, a star football player, a vet or a policeman. Instead, he gradually discovered drugs and alcohol, which came to form part of an unbreakable cycle in his adult life. He turned to booze and stimulants as a way to cope with difficult situations, including when his father, Glen, died in a car accident, although, exactly when that occurred is unclear due to the fact that Daniel is notoriously untruthful.

There were glimmers of hope in his periods of sobriety, when he held down a job or maintained a relationship. But those periods never lasted. And when he got into trouble he blamed his childhood for his behaviour. The theme was always the same — a disadvantaged upbringing that shaped him for a life of crime and drug abuse, a path he couldn't avoid.

Still, Daniel Holdom managed to form a relationship with a young woman in Orange. He'd met Kylie when they were both teenagers. They started dating, and soon he was a dad and husband. He promised himself he would never abuse the children.

'We got married, it was beautiful and I was so happy, I was so wrapped [sic] and proud,' Holdom wrote years later. 'Could not be happier having my son and daughter, so proud to be a dad.'

Kylie encouraged him to play football and Holdom viewed it as a distraction from drugs, alcohol and bad influences. The second-rower dreamt of playing professionally but a shoulder and hand injury forced him to quit. He saw the setback as a catastrophic derailment — another example of life serving him more than his fair share of struggle.

With their eyes on a fresh start, Holdom, Kylie and their two children moved to Coffs Harbour in 2001, but what became a familiar pattern soon emerged. Holdom picked up part-time work with Coastal Drilling, a firm that drilled for water and constructed bores in and around the hinterland of Coffs Harbour. Holdom threw himself into his work; he was diligent, punctual, and was set on studying for his own driller's licence. His boss, Robert Tanner, was a man well into his sixties, looking for a trustworthy and hardworking employee, and he thought he'd found that in Holdom.

'I have absolutely no problem with his attitude, honesty and workability,' Tanner said in a reference years later. 'When it comes to facing major or minor problems he has the ability to remain quite calm and sort things out before he makes any major move. This man is virtually indispensable ...'

This kind of support and encouragement was something Holdom had seldom experienced from a male figure in his life. However, it amounted to nothing when his personal life exploded and his drug abuse left Kylie fed up. She applied for an apprehended domestic violence order, which Holdom ignored. He was committing small-time frauds, passing valueless cheques in exchange for cash to feed his drug habit.

'She couldn't cope with it anymore,' Holdom wrote years later. 'She hated me using drugs. Most times I hid it but she would find out when money was spent and not in the bank.'

Holdom's marriage had completely broken down. Soon he was living in a caravan on his own on the semi-rural outskirts of town but was unwilling to accept the relationship was over. His temper flared and his behaviour swung wildly between that of a heartbroken father who just wanted to see his kids and an enraged, scorned ex-partner with an axe to grind.

On 15 August 2001, he turned up on the doorstep of Kylie's house in Coffs Harbour to beg her to take him back. When Kylie left to pick up their children from school and day-care, he followed, undeterred by her pleas to leave them alone. Outside the school, while laughing children ran towards their waiting parents, he hurled abuse at Kylie. As she hurried her son into the car, trying to ignore Holdom's taunts, mortified mothers watched sympathetically.

From there, Holdom stalked Kylie in his car, stopping and starting and driving dangerously close to her vehicle. She made it back home but Holdom blocked the driveway with his car and demanded to talk to her. He wanted a second chance to repair their fractured marriage, he pleaded. Fed up, Kylie headed towards Coffs Harbour Police Station, a move that finally sent Holdom running in the other direction.

When police eventually caught up with Holdom two days later, he was charged with breaching an AVO, but it had little effect. His appearances at court were sporadic. Magistrates issued arrest warrants for failing to appear but Holdom's transient lifestyle meant he was a hard man to track down. He either had little regard for the rule of law or was too far gone on drugs and alcohol to remember important dates. Eventually he was sentenced for AVO breaches, a reality check that forced him to sober up and reflect on his broken relationships.

'I know that I should have dealt with our conflicts differently, instead of yelling back at her for not letting me see my kids when it was my weekend to see them,' Holdom explained in a handwritten letter to a Coffs Harbour magistrate in early 2002. 'I know that I should have just walked away and reported it. At first all divorced couples have different conflicts, I just learned the hard way how to deal with problems.

'The last time I spoke to my ex-wife was when I rang her on Christmas Day for my kids to come over, as it was my turn. For the second half of the day I asked nicely and all I got was abuse and told if I rang again she would make accusations against me.

'My point is I did the right thing, I hung up and reported it. My ex-wife also rang up two days later claiming my son James is not mine. That she was tested at Coffs Harbour pathology a while ago and said that James is my brothers [sic] and you have been paying maintenance, ha ha! I then hung up and reported it to the police. Now if I can do the right thing in these two situations I can do the right thing in any future as a mature adult.'

Holdom lost contact with the two children he fathered with Kylie. He claimed he tried to change his ways; he organised counselling, stayed off the bottle for a few months and found love with a new woman. They even planned to get engaged.

Again, he was at a point in his life where the future looked hopeful and again he ruined any prospects of success by taking drugs. His then-girlfriend took out an AVO and he breached that when he assaulted her in 2003.

In around 2004, Holdom skipped town to Queensland, knowing the police were looking for him for a long list of offences — fraud, theft and breaching apprehended violence orders — and leaving a handful of shattered relationships in his wake. He travelled to Tin Can Bay, a sleepy, coastal hamlet surrounded by mangroves at the foot of Fraser Island, just north of Brisbane. There he moved into a share house with a friend and called himself Daniel Bishop.

It was in Tin Can Bay, in his friend's backyard on a humid New Year's Eve, that Holdom met Hazel Passmore, the woman whose little daughter, Lauryn, would later play with Khandalyce in the backyard of their home in Alice Springs.

Chapter 12

To Hazel Passmore, an overweight woman with wispy brown hair and almond-shaped eyes, Daniel Holdom was the bee's knees. He came across as charming, and when she brought him home to meet her mother he was a hit. Hazel thought Holdom didn't do drugs, didn't drink much, and held a stable job, which was more than she could say about her former partners. She was swept off her feet and she could tell Holdom was equally smitten.

Their arguments were explosive but their hold on one another was strong. Holdom's abusive childhood had taught him to trust no one, but Hazel seemed to get him like no other woman had. He told Hazel about his past — his traumatic upbringing, the neglect, the bashings — warts and all. Later, he would describe Hazel as supportive and their relationship stable. They knew each other's darkest secrets, their most shameful memories, and they shared in fantasies other people never would have understood.

Even though Hazel disapproved of Holdom's involvement in crime (he'd brought his fraudulent behaviours with him to Queensland), she understood the difficulties he faced 'behaviourally, emotionally and legally' and she attributed those issues to his childhood.

Still, despite hitting it off with Hazel, Holdom eventually skipped town for New South Wales, where he was arrested for passing fraudulent cheques and sparking a false police investigation that involved a bogus plot by bikies to kill a police officer. The latter scheme was an attempt to curry favour with the police to get a softer sentence for his outstanding charges.

As it turned out, Holdom spent eight months behind bars. All the while, Hazel was on his mind. When finally he was released in the mid 2000s, he learned she had a baby girl named Lauryn. Holdom would tell people the baby was his but Hazel later claimed Lauryn was the child of an ex-boyfriend, with whom she had two other children — Willow and Ryan.

Fresh on parole, Holdom turned up at Hazel's house in the middle of the night and convinced her to pack up her life, pull her kids out of school and move to Taree, 830 kilometres away. Holdom had roots in the area but it was a trigger for mixed emotions: his grandparents still lived there, as did his beloved now-late aunt, and it was where he'd reconnected with his father, Glen, before he died. But it was also a reminder of the relatives who had washed their hands of him when he was a child. Regardless, he figured it was a nice place to settle in for a while until he decided his next move.

The couple rented a house near the Twilight Caravan Park, a sprawling camping ground just south of the town that was popular with grey nomads travelling the Pacific Highway from Sydney to Queensland. The owner of the house also owned the caravan park, and in mid 2007, he cut Hazel and Holdom a deal. The man wanted to sell his caravan but needed someone to do it for him. If Hazel and Holdom would keep an eye out for interested purchasers, and if they did the haggling on his behalf, they could keep the proceeds over $2000.

On the morning of 11 May 2007, Ken Lavender stopped to look at the blue and turquoise caravan with a For Sale sign on the back windscreen that was parked outside the house Holdom and Hazel were staying in. Holdom met Ken outside, his hand outstretched, with Hazel following closely behind him.

Ken poked his head around the caravan; it wasn't in pristine condition and needed a bit of work. Sensing his hesitation, Holdom offered to wipe $900 off the sale price; it was Ken's for $1500.

Ken placed a wad of cash into his hand. Hazel whipped out a receipt book and began recording Ken's details, providing him with a false sense of legitimacy, then scribbled out a receipt for $1500.

Hazel's boyfriend had a wad of fifty dollar notes in his hand — more money than they'd had in a while, and it had all been so easy.

Ken wanted to take his new caravan straightaway but couldn't risk towing it 100 kilometres north up the Pacific Highway in case the police pulled him over. He'd have to fix up the registration back home in Kempsey then return to collect the caravan. Holdom agreed that was a wise idea.

Chuffed by his efforts and with a little more confidence, Holdom pulled off the same manoeuvre with another buyer the next day. That time he pocketed $1200 in cash.

Both duped buyers tried Holdom's mobile number over the following days but their calls went unanswered. They turned up at the house looking for him, but the house was empty and the caravan missing.

By then, Holdom and Hazel were cruising down the east coast, pockets lined with cash and discussing where they should go next. Only two weeks earlier, Holdom and a mate had pinched copper offcuts and insulated wire from a scrap metal yard in Taree and had cashed it in for $1900 in Sydney.

Hazel was now part of Holdom's transient lifestyle, traversing the rural highways between the ACT, South Australia, Victoria and the Northern Territory with the three kids. They wanted to show the children the real Australia, they told themselves — the dry, orange plains, empty highways and tiny country towns that Holdom could drift in and out of without notice. He later claimed he'd saved up $10,000 to fund the trip around Australia by working hard, but he failed to disclose how much of that had come from theft and fraud.

In mid 2007, the family was in South Australia and running out of money. A busted fan belt brought the trip to a halt in Roxby Downs, a modern mining town popular with families who need a place to call home while husbands and fathers go to work in the opal mines nearby. Hazel, Holdom and the kids stayed at a caravan park for fifteen weeks, putting away part of their welfare payments and income from odd jobs each week until they saved enough money to get going north again.

The next stop was Alice Springs. The town's status as the gateway to Australia's iconic landmark, Uluru, draws hundreds of thousands of visitors through the town every year. They come to see the towering rocky outcrops and the kangaroos that gather on the town's fringes, and to pick up a souvenir tea towel or toy koala from one of the many souvenir shops.

For Holdom, Alice was the ideal place to get lost. No one would know about his past; no one could judge him on his failings.

'I was away from all bad influences,' Holdom wrote years later. 'We both had good jobs. After twelve months though I started with drugs again.'

Chapter 13

Hazel and Holdom had been living in Alice Springs for almost a year. On 15 September 2008, a few days out from Ryan's eighth birthday, they set off for Adelaide for a weekend with the three kids.

The family was making the long trip in a rental four-wheel-drive because Holdom's car had been almost written off weeks earlier. Reports differed on who was at fault: Holdom claimed Hazel deliberately smashed the car into a tree because she didn't want him to do a drug run; Hazel claimed Holdom crashed the car after one of his endless nights out. It was indicative of their relationship, a cycle of lies and deceit.

The Stuart Highway cuts a swathe across the marbled, lunar landscape surrounding Alice Springs. The arterial road that connects the town to capital cities north and south makes for a dull drive, the straight single carriageway seeming to stretch on forever without a dwelling or sign of life in sight.

It was a long drive to Adelaide — fifteen hours — but Holdom, behind the wheel, was feeling alert. He'd driven the road many times before, picking up drugs from a warehouse in South Australia and couriering them back to Alice Springs. Years later he would claim Hazel had no idea about his drug use, even though he plied his trade from their home.

Holdom's drug use had increased exponentially to the point where he was taking a gram of ice at a time. Most users smoke ice in a pipe or inject it into their veins, but Holdom ate it, a habit that left his mouth ravaged with ulcers and stripped weight from his towering frame. (He would later tell police it was so he could stay awake to finish all the work he was getting through his private car-detailing business.)

Two days earlier, Holdom had used methamphetamine but didn't believe for a minute it would impair his driving skills. He enjoyed the familiar feeling of euphoria that washed over him when the drug pulsed through his veins. It helped him forget the traumas that plagued his life and left him feeling indestructible.

Holdom later claimed that he began smoking speed at twenty-six, had moved onto a three-month ecstasy binge, and then took up methamphetamines. He used the drugs to 'escape' and avoid dealing with unwanted thoughts, memories and emotions, including those linked to his abusive childhood.

By the time Holdom and Hazel had bundled Willow, Ryan and Lauryn into the back of the car, the effects of the drug had well and truly weakened. Or so he thought.

They'd made good progress by nightfall, crossing the border into South Australia, where they decided to take a rest stop. Everyone climbed out of the car. It was pitch black but clear and stars blanketed the night sky. Holdom sparked up a cigarette and stood on the roadside as the kids went to the toilet a few metres away. Willow and Ryan skipped back to the four-wheel-drive and clambered into the back seat. Holdom later said that he clicked their seatbelts in, gave them a kiss on the forehead and said, 'I love you.'

'I resumed driving on,' he recalled in a handwritten letter found in his prison records years later. 'Half an hour later, 50km north of Marla, there were roos all over the road. I swerved to go around them and the car rolled. I was so terrified and horrified by what I saw next that night.'

Minutes before 10 pm, not far from Indulkana, a speck on the map in the northern reaches of South Australia where the highway slices the flat, red, rocky earth in half, the car veered sharply off the road. It flipped several times before landing on the roof in the middle of the desert.

The sounds of a hissing engine and glass cracking stirred Holdom and the smell of petrol fumes burned his nostrils. Hazel was still in the passenger seat, strained against her seatbelt. Holdom's twisted around. He could see Lauryn, aged two, in the booster seat, blood dripping from a small cut on her forehead, but Willow, nine, and Ryan, seven, weren't there.

Holdom crawled out of the mangled four-wheel-drive to find the children sprawled on the dirt. They weren't moving and he realised what he'd done. Holdom sat in the dark in the desert next to his stepchildren's lifeless bodies, waiting for help to arrive.

Nurses from Marla — a rural community with a health centre run by the Royal Flying Doctor Service — arrived within an hour and found Holdom attempting to render first aid to Hazel. Her injuries were severe; both her knees were dislocated, she had a compound fracture to her left knee and extensive soft tissue degloving — her skin had been ripped back on itself, exposing tendons and bone. She needed to be treated at a major trauma centre, and was airlifted from Alice Springs Hospital to the Royal Adelaide Hospital where she was placed in an induced coma for two weeks.

Hazel underwent surgery after surgery as doctors attempted to save her legs, but a serious infection forced surgeons to amputate her left leg above the knee. Her right knee was placed in a long cast and treated with skin grafts and muscle flaps. She would be confined to a wheelchair for the rest of her life. She also underwent a bowel resection to treat major abdominal injuries.

Holdom suffered a broken collarbone and thumb but was released from hospital a day after the crash. A security guard at Alice Springs Hospital reported taking tens of thousands of dollars in cash off Holdom when he was admitted. He claimed it had been legitimately earned but police suspected it was to buy drugs in South Australia.

After he was discharged, Holdom travelled between Alice Springs and Adelaide to be by Hazel's hospital bedside, sometimes stopping at the scene of the crash to look for body parts the police might have missed in the aftermath. One day he claimed he found a piece of his daughter's skull and marched into Marla Police Station with it, demanding officers go back to the accident site and clean it up properly.

In minute and graphic detail, like a form of self-torture, Holdom relived the crash over and over again in his head. The sight of his daughter's bloodied face followed him in his dreams and he used drugs as an easy way out of the despair.

'Mr Marshall [the alias he was charged under] reported experiencing a range of symptoms, which included insomnia ... guilt, feeling worthless, that life is hopeless, anxiety, hyper-vigilance, de-realisation, flashbacks and numbness of feelings,' a psychologist would later report. '... [D]espite feeling constantly anxious and tired, he has difficulty falling asleep and sleeping for any length of time but "keeps going".'

Holdom blamed himself for killing Willow and Ryan, and so did the police. They were slowly building a case against him after traces of methamphetamine were detected in a drug and alcohol test immediately after the crash.

In Alice Springs the community mourned for Ryan and Willow. An article from the *Northern Territory News*, published in September 2008, stated:

Two Alice Springs children who were killed in a car accident last week have been remembered as much-loved students, and counselling has been provided to their teachers and school friends at Gillen Primary.

Gillen Primary assistant principal Lyndsay Thomas said the school community was 'saddened by the sudden passing of our much loved students'.

She said, 'Willow and Ryan will be missed by us all. Our thoughts are with their family'.

Holdom felt the pressure bearing down on him, and that all too familiar urge crept up on him again. It was like an itch he couldn't scratch, a niggling he couldn't ignore. He had to escape.

Chapter 14

It was a warm day in late 2008, and the first time Hazel had been allowed out of the Royal Adelaide Hospital since waking up from two weeks in a coma after the car crash. Hazel was relieved to be out of the sanitised hospital ward and away from the overly attentive nurses and endless examinations.

Holdom had promised hospital staff he would only take her as far as the shopping precinct — where Hazel's sister, Amanda, and her partner, Chris, were waiting — and that he'd return her in a couple of hours.

As Holdom pushed her down the mall, Hazel's vulnerability was laid bare. She had never been so dependent on him. She appreciated his effort to give her a reprieve from the hospital ward but she was still reeling from what Holdom had done. Every time she looked at him, she was reminded of her children.

In early October, she'd woken up in intensive care and learned that her son, Ryan, a few days shy of his eighth birthday, and daughter Willow had died instantly in the car accident that had also robbed her of her mobility. Her wails had filled the sterile hospital halls and immediately she blamed Holdom. He'd been behind the wheel; it was his responsibility to protect them, to get them to Adelaide in one piece. She screamed at him when he turned up at her hospital bedside, an anger that only intensified when she heard that Karlie and Khandalyce were with him.

Attempting to pacify her, Holdom said Karlie was only there to see Hazel, but Hazel didn't buy it. From the beginning of her friendship with Karlie, Hazel had found herself comparing her life, her role as a mother and as a girlfriend, to Karlie. Perhaps it was jealousy or mere observation, but Hazel also couldn't help comparing Karlie's daughter with her own. Every time Khandalyce turned up at her house she had a new outfit on — a black tutu with polka dots or a cute pink cotton dress — colours that complemented her glossy shoulder-length blonde hair. In contrast, Lauryn, as the youngest of three children, was dressed in hand-me-downs and her head was shaved, a drastic measure to stop her pulling her hair out.

Now, most likely at Holdom's invitation, Karlie had come to Adelaide to see Hazel on her first outing from hospital. Hazel watched the dynamic between Karlie and Holdom as they strolled down North Terrace, past the city's bustling railway station before turning towards Rundle Mall. Hazel would later claim that Holdom had bought Karlie a tight-fitting mini-skirt that hugged her slender frame and showed off her slim legs. Seated in her wheelchair with a flowing skirt hiding her amputated leg, Hazel felt uncomfortable.

Seizing on a moment alone with her sister, Amanda, Hazel asked if there was anything going on between Holdom and Karlie. Amanda had been staying at the same motel while Hazel remained in hospital; if sparks were flying, she would have noticed. However, Amanda assured her everything was fine.

The truth was, as Hazel said later, Amanda didn't think her sister could handle her boyfriend playing up on her on top of the trauma she'd experienced. A month earlier, Hazel had been an inch from death. She had survived her catastrophic injuries but her mental and physical recovery was paramount, so Amanda was keeping quiet.

Nevertheless, the unnerving, sinking feeling in Hazel's stomach lingered. Karlie's ex-boyfriend, Robbie, had been calling Hazel, asking where Karlie was. 'I don't know, fucking ask Daniel,' she'd reply, knowing full well Karlie was in Adelaide. And it didn't seem like she was returning to Alice Springs anytime soon.

Hazel watched Holdom and Karlie throughout the day but kept her thoughts to herself until she reached the hospital. When Karlie was out of earshot, Hazel's fury erupted in an expletive-laden tirade that culminated in a stern warning — Karlie wasn't to go anywhere near Willow's and Ryan's funeral, which was in a few days.

The service on 14 November 2008, was marked with great sadness as Hazel laid her two children to rest at a funeral chapel in Hillcrest in South Australia. The following day, after releasing balloons into the sky, a message from Holdom appeared on Hazel's phone. The police were after him, the message read, he had to leave.

Holdom grovelled for her understanding, texting lie after lie in a feeble attempt to justify his sudden disappearance. 'The police are going to find me' and 'I had no other choice'.

Hazel would later say she came to learn that Holdom was a pathological liar: 'You couldn't believe a word that came out of his mouth.'

Karlie, her daughter and her maroon-coloured station wagon were gone too. The pain Hazel was already feeling amplified. More than anything, she was furious. Furious that her boyfriend would leave her in the state she was in, and furious that her friend Karlie would leave with him.

In text messages, Holdom claimed he wasn't with Karlie in a romantic sense and that they were just visiting his family in the ACT to escape police attention, but Hazel didn't believe him. She fired dozens of text messages off to Karlie, calling her a 'slut, a bitch, a skank, a home wrecker'. Karlie replied that she wasn't doing what Hazel suspected, but that did little to calm Hazel down — she felt utterly betrayed.

Not long after Holdom left Adelaide, he sent Hazel a picture of a police car. It was a flimsy attempt to convince Hazel that the police were actually after him, but it backfired when Hazel spotted a blonde-haired young girl in the corner of the image. There was no denying it was Khandalyce, even though Holdom swore black and blue that it wasn't. The image only cemented in Hazel's mind that Holdom had left her for Karlie.

As the hospital bills mounted, Hazel reached out to a lawyer at Slater and Gordon; she was going to sue Holdom for the personal injury, loss and damage caused as a result of the fatal accident. According to Hazel's statement of claim lodged in the District Court of South Australia, Holdom was negligent in failing to keep a proper lookout, to brake in time to avoid the collision, and that he drove at excessive speed.

While Hazel was unemployed at the time of the crash, the accident had reduced her ability to work and left her with ongoing pain. The damages she sought would have covered loss of superannuation benefits, medical costs, loss of earning capacity, future car and gardening services, travel costs, and home modifications to accommodate her wheelchair.

According to the statement of claim, Hazel had been discharged from the Royal Adelaide Hospital and transferred to the Hampstead Rehabilitation Centre in November 2008. However she'd had to be readmitted to hospital due to a severe infection in her right thigh. She was finally discharged in December, when she was moved back to the rehabilitation centre, from where she sent a series of accusatory messages to Holdom. In a cunning move, she subtly mentioned the looming civil suit she had in the works. In a small way, it was satisfying to get one up on her former partner.

Almost immediately, the apologetic tone in his text messages changed and he began to hint at a return to Adelaide to reunite with Hazel. He made a mistake, he claimed, and he wanted to see his daughter again. He yearned for forgiveness and spoke of returning in time for Christmas to bring Lauryn toys.

Deep down, Hazel suspected that it was the threat of her lawsuit that had caused Holdom to change his mind, not his undying love for her. It would eventually fall to Holdom's compulsory third-party insurer to pay out whatever settlement was reached, but Hazel surmised Holdom thought he could share in the money if they were an item again. As someone who grew up stealing food to survive, Holdom seized any opportunity to make cash.

Hazel's phone buzzed constantly throughout the day on 19 December 2008, Holdom was making his way back to her in Adelaide, and while she later claimed to be nonchalant about his return, her actions suggested otherwise.

She'd stayed with her sister at the Cancer Council Lodge in Greenhill before Disability SA helped find a transitional unit on Hargrave Street in Northfield on the northern outskirts of Adelaide. It was close to the Hampstead Rehabilitation Centre and the rent was heavily subsidised for eighteen months until she could find a permanent place to live.

Hazel said later that on 19 December, the day she moved into the unit, she learned Holdom was coming home. Anticipating his arrival that night, she went to the local supermarket and bought ingredients for dinner.

Every few hours she received a call from him with updates on how far away he was. Finally, at 2:06 am on 20 December, several hours later than he'd estimated and his dinner now cold, Holdom pulled into the driveway of Hazel's new unit complex. He was driving a white Holden Statesman, a car Hazel had never seen before. As he recited the all-too-familiar line about police chasing him, he appeared scattered, almost incoherent.

Holdom pleaded for help with his trauma and, in the end, Hazel relented. She resented him for abandoning her, but in her vulnerable state she felt relieved that normalcy returned to her life when he walked through the front door. Here was someone who would love her even with her disability, even if it was a love based on convenience or greed. So she let him into her life again.

Chapter 15

As soon as Karlie and Khandals had walked out of her mother's front door with the man called Daniel, Colleen and Tanya had discussed the bad feeling they had about him.

'What was that all about?' Tanya asked. She wondered what Karlie would be doing with a guy who looked the same age as her stepfather.

Colleen was equally confused but her daughter was a big girl; she had the right to make her own decisions and learn from them. Yet it was impossible for Colleen to hide her concern when Scott arrived home from work to the news his stepdaughter had left town. 'When I got home, Col was a bit upset, and I put it down to a mother's instinct. It's almost like she didn't trust him at all,' he later recalled.

Then, about a week or so later, Tanya's phone rang. It was Karlie and she was crying hysterically.

'I've fucked up,' she told Tanya between shaky breaths.

Instantly worried, Tanya hit Karlie with a string of questions — where was she, who was she with, what had she fucked up?

Karlie wouldn't give her a straight answer but it was clear, once Tanya managed to calm her down, that she wanted to come home.

Karlie hinted at returning but was confused about where to go. She felt like she couldn't go back to her mum and dad's place, she said, because Scott was upset with her for leaving town.

It seemed like such an over-exaggerated concern compared to Karlie's emotional state. Her parents loved her and would get over whatever spat they might have had, Tanya assured her. Besides, Karlie could always stay at her house, as she had in the past.

'Are you safe?' Tanya asked. 'Tell me where you are?'

Tanya offered to arrange for a friend to pick Karlie up, but as the conversation went on, Karlie's desperation to return home seemed to dissipate. And her mood softened. Perhaps it was the familiar voice that put her at ease.

By the end of the conversation, Karlie's tone had changed; she sounded happy and chuckled at Tanya's jokes.

'I thought maybe she just needed reassurance,' Tanya recalled later.

Every other phone call Tanya made to Karlie's phone after that day was unanswered.

***

On 13 December Colleen received a phone call from Karlie, but then Christmas came and went without a call or even a text. Colleen had hoped Karlie and Khandals would come home for the occasion and the lack of contact left her unnerved and annoyed. It was extremely unusual. Until

Karlie left, Karlie and Colleen had spoken every day and Christmas was a big family affair for the Poveys.

Karlie wasn't Colleen's only worry. She'd been diagnosed with breast cancer earlier that year and had started chemotherapy. While Colleen underwent the treatment, the family was reduced to one income and Scott often worked away. Without a second thought, Tanya had stepped in to take Colleen to her appointments with oncologists at Flinders Medical Centre in Adelaide. The conversation between the two friends on the flights between the Red Centre and South Australia's capital city regularly turned to Karlie's sudden and painful silence.

Then, a few days after Christmas, just before New Year's Eve, Robbie received a message from Karlie. She was in Adelaide, she said, sleeping in her car with Khandalyce, with no place to stay. Concerned, and with Khandalyce forefront in his mind, Robbie sent through the address of his parents, who lived in Adelaide and said they should go and stay at his family's home — he didn't want them out on the street.

On another occasion, Robbie received another text from Karlie, suggesting she was broke and stuck in Tennant Creek, a tiny town 500 kilometres north of Alice Springs. Again Robbie stepped in to help. When Karlie sent through her bank account details, it was a different account from the one she'd used in the past. Days then weeks passed, but Karlie didn't come home.

While calls to Karlie's phone went unanswered, her family and a few friends did receive text messages during 2009.

In February, Ray received a message from Karlie. Ray had already done a bit of digging about Daniel, and before long had learned about the car crash he'd caused.

'What's Karlie doing, going with a bloke that has left a woman who lost a leg?' Ray said to her mum, Connie. 'What sort of bloke is he? Does Karlie know he's done this?'

When Karlie went to ground, Connie, Ray and Sharon tried to get in contact with her. When messages from Karlie's phone came through in 2009, it seemed she was content with a new life in Queensland but wanted to be left alone.

Ray replied, telling Karlie her family loved and missed her. That message went unanswered.

In around June 2009, Robbie received another text message from Karlie saying she couldn't afford a present for Khandalyce's birthday. Would he lend her some money?

Then, on Karlie's twenty-first birthday on 7 August, Scott received a text message from his daughter's mobile phone. 'It's my 21st birthday today. Don't you care about me anymore?' the text read. The spelling was poor and while Karlie was an avid texter — 'she could text with her phone behind her back' and was a whiz with acronyms — the language and tone of the message didn't sound like her.

Scott replied anyway, wishing her a happy birthday and reminding her that she was the one who left the family home.

He never received a reply.

During the first half of 2009, Colleen had received a string of text messages from Karlie's phone, requesting money, but by September 2009 the contact had dwindled to nothing.

Calls went to voicemail or didn't connect at all and Karlie's Facebook hadn't been used in months. Tanya and Colleen discussed possible theories, some more far-fetched than others, to explain Karlie's lack of communication. Maybe she was heavily involved in drugs and was embarrassed to come home. Maybe this Daniel guy was controlling her. They reached a point where they couldn't bear to sit around and discuss the frightening what-ifs anymore.

'We were both trying to ring her all the time from different phones, just to make sure she wasn't avoiding us,' Tanya said later. 'It got to the point where we thought, all right let's do it. So we marched down to Alice Springs Police Station with a photo of Karlie.'

More than 38,000 people are reported missing in Australia every year. Most turn up safe and well — teenage runaways who sheepishly return home ready to make up with their parents after a few nights couch surfing; or travellers who finally make contact with their worried relatives overseas.

Fewer than thirty turn out to be genuinely 'missing', that is, people who don't turn up after three months.

Therefore, consciously or subconsciously, police tend to assume that a missing person will turn up one way or another.

On 4 September 2009, at Colleen's request, Northern Territory Police opened a missing persons report for Karlie Pearce-Stevenson. Colleen provided an officer at Alice Springs Police Station with a photograph of Karlie and said that her daughter had left the town in November 2008 with Daniel Marshall.

Three days later, on 7 September 2009, an officer contacted Daniel, who was in Adelaide at the time, on his mobile phone and asked if he had seen Karlie.

Daniel claimed he hadn't, not since Karlie had contacted him earlier that year. Last he heard, he said, Karlie was living with another man in Queensland. He told the officer he thought he had her mobile somewhere and promised to try and find it and call straight back.

Daniel never did call back, and follow-up phone calls went unanswered. Police also contacted the Australian Central Credit Union, where Karlie had a bank account, to check if there had been any recent activity, which is standard procedure in a missing person investigation.

Karlie's account had been used regularly, and as recently as 7 September, and Northern Territory Police took this as a sign she was alive.

Police also did a search for the whereabouts of Karlie's car, and discovered the Holden Commodore had been traded in at a car dealership in Canberra. Someone called Dereck Dover was on the paperwork.

The Northern Territory Police report stated that Dover, when asked about Karlie, claimed he'd dropped her at a bus stop in December 2008 and that had been the last he saw of her.

In the police version of events, unearthed years later, an officer told Colleen that Karlie's bank account had been accessed but that the missing persons investigation would remain open until Karlie was physically seen or spoken to. Then, on 10 September 2009, Northern Territory Police claimed that Colleen had called and requested that the missing person's report be closed because she'd heard from her daughter. According to police, on 10 September 2009, Colleen had received a phone call from someone claiming to be Karlie. It had been difficult to hear the caller's raspy voice whispering down the phone line but 'Karlie' said she was safe and didn't want to speak with her family.

However, Scott and Tanya dispute this version of events. They recalled that Northern Territory Police contacted Colleen by phone when she was at home with Tanya, and said a police officer had spoken to Karlie, who was in

Victoria. Karlie had told the officer she was fine but didn't want to speak with her family. As a result, police would be closing the missing person's report.

Tanya distinctly remembered the disappointment on Colleen's face as she hung up the phone, and she accompanied her friend to the police station to pick up the photograph of Karlie.

Scott also recalled the conversation he had with Colleen that day. 'When I got home that afternoon, she had the photos and the report,' he said years later.

When detectives reviewed the Northern Territory Police missing person's report six years later, they were critical of the decision to close the investigation without physically sighting Karlie. The failure to obtain a proof of life and the reliance on Karlie's bank account activity had given her family hope that she was alive.

Chapter 16

2012

The insidious illness had stalked Colleen for four years. She knew it would come to this; the most recent prognosis had been that it was terminal.

In an Alice Springs palliative care unit, Scott held her hand and put on a brave face when she repeated the question he couldn't bear to answer.

'Are Karlie and Khandals here yet?'

Back in 2008, when Colleen had been diagnosed with an aggressive form of breast cancer, Scott had waited until his wife was out of earshot before sneaking back into the specialist's office for the honest truth. He was a no-bullshit kind of man who wanted it straight — how bad was it?

One year at best, he was told.

Colleen had staved off breast cancer for four years, unwilling to let it beat her. She'd had a mastectomy and been through rounds of chemotherapy but the cancer had spread to her lungs.

Still she held on longer than doctors had estimated. Something gave her the will to live. She yearned to find her daughter and granddaughter.

Since the missing person's report had been closed in 2009, irregular text messages and calls from Karlie continued.

On 11 September 2010, after Colleen had undergone an operation as part of her cancer treatment and was recovering in an Adelaide hospital, she received a text message from Karlie. According to Tanya, the message stated that Karlie was living in Noosa Heads and needed money.

Colleen had also received another phone call, in either 2010 or 2011, from Karlie's phone. The female voice sounded muffled and explained that she was hiding from someone and had two phones.

Colleen's sister, Sharon, would tell police that Colleen deposited $500 into Karlie's account in January 2009, after Karlie called her from a pay phone in Queensland. Karlie claimed she was in Mount Isa and needed money to travel to Alice Springs. In September that year — five days after the missing person's report was closed — Colleen deposited another $500 into Karlie's bank account. Without telling Scott, Colleen, ecstatic at the thought her daughter and granddaughter were finally coming home, would transfer money after each request, even if it was the last bit of cash they had left at the time.

Scott suspected these loans to Karlie were being blown on drugs and was not happy when he discovered the money missing from their account.

And when Karlie never came home, Scott's confusion turned to anger. He began to wonder what he and Colleen had done wrong. What was so bad that Karlie couldn't come home? Karlie knew before she left Alice Springs that her mother had found a lump in her breast but the only times she heard from Karlie was when she needed money. It felt selfish and careless.

And when Karlie's grandmother, Connie, died in

September 2011, Karlie didn't return for the funeral. Her absence infuriated her stepfather even more.

Now, Colleen lay in palliative care, heavily medicated. The doctors suggested that Scott and Tanya get Colleen's affairs in order because they didn't know how much time she had left. Then a nurse pulled Tanya aside and mentioned that Colleen had asked after Karlie and Khandalyce a number of times. The dying woman had posed the same question to Tanya, Scott and her sisters, Ray and Sharon, when they came to visit her in the ward. Where was Karlie? And when was she coming home?

During her final days, Colleen hallucinated that Karlie and Khandalyce were standing in the corner of the room.

As the family prepared for the inevitable, Ray went into Alice Springs Police Station and asked an officer to try and get in contact with Karlie. Her mother was about to die and the family wanted her to be at the funeral.

According to Ray, the police tried unsuccessfully to find Karlie, but she was no longer living at her last-known address and phone calls to her last-known boyfriend, Daniel Holdom, went unanswered.

On 6 February 2012, at forty-four years of age, Colleen died without knowing what had become of her daughter and granddaughter.

'I was holding her hand when she died and I knew then Karlie was not coming,' Scott said years later.

* * *

October 2015

The pink child's coat, with the faux fur around the collar, seemed familiar to Tanya. She'd spotted the distinctive jacket while reading a news story about child's bones found in a suitcase in Wynarka in South Australia. Other images caught her attention too: a pair of purple silk boxer shorts with a teddy bear print, pink girls' pants and Holden-branded shorts.

As she read through story after story, Tanya found herself in tears in front of the computer. She couldn't help but think of Karlie and Khandalyce. Since the young mother and daughter had left Alice Springs almost seven years earlier, Tanya had thought of them often, wondering where they were and how they were doing. Khandals would be nine by now, Tanya would think, and probably looked just like her mum: slim, fair, with brown eyes.

Now Tanya was uneasy, a feeling that only intensified following a day spent with Karlie's stepfather, Scott. After the death of her best friend, Colleen, Tanya had eventually left Alice Springs and settled in Darwin, where she'd set up a business from home with her husband, Michael. Coincidentally, Colleen's widower, Scott, had moved to Darwin too, and the two old friends had simply picked up from where they'd left off.

On 3 October 2015, they'd caught up for a few drinks at a local pub on the afternoon of the AFL grand final. In the early evening, Tanya and Scott's new partner, Brenda, retired to Scott and Brenda's balcony overlooking a glistening bay in Darwin's west while the men had one last beer in town. The images Tanya had seen of the clothing in the suitcase were playing on her mind and she discussed her niggling fears with Brenda. While Brenda, a compassionate and warm woman, hadn't met the missing mother and child, she knew that their absence had caused Scott's family enormous pain.

'Karlie used to dress Khandals in boxer shorts when she was hot. She'd run around with them over her nappy,' Tanya said. She also pointed out that Khandalyce fitted the description of the unidentified child — two-and-a-half to four years old, blonde hair, Caucasian.

Scott had recognised the coat too, Brenda said, and had spent hours poring over news stories about the Wynarka investigation. Then he'd spoken to his sisters, who'd remarked that a unique quilt found in the suitcase looked exactly like the quilt Scott's late mother had given to Khandalyce after she was born.

In a bid to put his racing mind at ease, Scott had told Brenda he'd go to a police station and report the names of Karlie and Khandalyce. Hopefully, the police would rule out Khandalyce as a potential victim and confirm that his suspicions were far-fetched. Karlie and Khandalyce would still be missing but it was more comforting than the alternative.

But when the Wynarka case broke, Scott was working out of Adelaide, overseeing a huge logistics operation. He'd been working around the clock and when a colleague's son died unexpectedly, his workload increased. In short, he'd not managed to get down to a police station.

As Tanya listened to Brenda relay Scott's concerns, she decided she needed to categorically rule out the possibility that the girl in the suitcase was Khandalyce. The following morning, she would call Crime Stoppers and put forward the toddler's name.

But while she'd made the decision, following through proved much more challenging. It felt like a physically impossible task. Every time she picked up the phone, she put it down again, convinced she was overreacting.

Sure, Khandalyce had similar clothing but it was all mass produced. Hundreds of other children probably had the same coat and boxer shorts.

As for the quilt, another family could've picked it up at a second-hand shop. She knew Karlie was planning to travel to Adelaide or Melbourne, and there had also been whispers she was in Queensland in recent years. Karlie could've dumped that quilt in any town during her travels.

It took another restless night's sleep for Tanya to make the call. Finally, on 6 October, she dialled the number. She got through.

After hanging up the phone, Tanya spoke to Brenda. Concerned about causing Scott unnecessary grief over an unconfirmed hunch, they decided to hold off telling him until they knew more. If it turned out to be true, he'd be the first to know, but, until then, they didn't see the benefit in worrying him further.

As she waited for a follow-up phone call from South Australia Police, Tanya searched nervously for evidence that might link Khandalyce to the suitcase. On finding a USB stick that had once belonged to Colleen, she plugged it into her computer and began trawling through old photographs of happier times in Alice Springs.

A series of photos of Khandalyce appeared and she stopped and hovered the cursor over them. They were clearly all taken at the same time, and were of Khandals in a black headband and a dusty pink dress with faint stripes. In all the photos the little girl was holding onto a pram.

Tanya's stomach dropped. Pulling up an internet browser, she punched the words 'Wynarka' and 'suitcase' into a search engine and waited. She found what she was looking for, a photo of a tiny, pink dress with faint stripes and cap sleeves laid out beside a forensic ruler.

Tanya placed the photo of the clothing and the photo of Khandalyce side by side on her screen. The dresses were identical.

It had been twenty-four hours since Tanya had contacted Crime Stoppers and she hadn't heard anything. So when police still hadn't been in contact the following day, 8 October, she contacted them again and said she had photos she needed to send them.

That night Detective Sergeant Blake Horder, from the Major Crime Investigation Branch, called Tanya and asked her to email the photographs to him.

She did, and less than an hour later, Horder rang to say the police had tracked Karlie and Khandalyce and they were alive and well. Relieved, she sent Brenda a message updating her on the development. But as Tanya got into bed that evening the old frustration returned: why hadn't Karlie called her family?

The following morning Tanya found a new email from Horder and she was instantly alarmed. The email contained a list of detailed questions about Karlie and Khandalyce. In her response, Tanya asked whether Karlie had been found. Horder rang an hour later to confirm that police had not located Karlie as they'd first thought.

The sick feeling in Tanya's stomach returned and she forwarded Horder's emails to Brenda.

Brenda decided it was time to tell Scott what was going on.

When he heard about the Crime Stoppers report, Scott contacted his two sisters again and asked if they'd had any luck finding photographs of Khandalyce.

Scott's older sister, Sue, distinctively remembered the unique quilt her mother had given Khandalyce during a visit to Adelaide in 2007. It was the last blanket her mother had made before she died of cancer in December that year. Like the rest of her family, Sue had long wondered what had happened to Karlie and Khandalyce.

The last she'd heard from her niece was around November 2008 when Karlie texted to say she was in Adelaide and wanted to drop by for a visit. Sue had heard that Karlie was keeping some unsavoury company, but she would never have denied her request. It was the people Karlie would turn up with that Sue was worried about. As it turned out, the next day Karlie changed her mind but reassured her aunty that they'd catch up soon.

During the years that followed, Sue bore witness to Colleen's unwavering hope that Karlie and Khandals would one day return. When Colleen was in Adelaide for medical treatment, she often stayed with Sue and they'd discuss the latest contact from Karlie. It was always a text message, never a phone call. More often than not, it was a request for money so Karlie could buy petrol or fix her car so she could make it home. 'This time she means it,' Colleen would assure Sue.

After Scott's request for photographs of Khandalyce, Sue found herself rifling through cupboards looking for the familiar quilt. Sue had moved into the family home after her mother died and had many of her old blankets.

She didn't find the quilt, but she did find a photograph of Khandalyce, sitting in a stroller with the distinctive quilt behind her. The top third of the photograph showed the multi-coloured musical notes that made up the quilt's unique edges.

Sue's daughter had taken the photograph inside their home during Karlie and Khandalyce's visit in 2007.

'I sent the photograph to my brother,' Sue recalled later. 'We were dumb struck. We didn't know where to go or where to turn.'

Scott compared the photograph against the image of the quilt found in the suitcase. There was no doubt the fabric matched. It was a sobering moment and all but confirmed to Scott that the little girl in the suitcase he had been reading about was the granddaughter he had been looking for.

He knew he'd seen the clothing before but it was the quilt, made by his mother in the same way she carefully sewed his clothing as a young boy, that was the missing piece of the puzzle.

On 11 October, Scott emailed the photograph of his granddaughter's blanket to Horder.

The following day, when they still haven't heard back, Sue called Crime Stoppers. 'I think I have some information on the child in the suitcase in Wynarka,' she told the operator. 'We found a picture and we believe it's the quilt they have been looking for.'

Unbeknownst to Sue, since Tanya's call detectives had been sourcing Khandalyce's medical records and organising a DNA comparison.

On 12 October, two detectives from the Major Crime Investigation Branch turned up at Sue's home. They sat around the dining table, dialled Scott's number and put the mobile phone on loudspeaker.

As Sue listened to Detective Amanda Bridge, she knew her brother's heart was breaking.

'I'm really sorry to say, but it is Khandalyce.'

Part III

Investigation

Chapter 17

At the request of police, for nine days Scott and his partner, Brenda, had kept the terrible secret that Khandalyce was the little girl in the suitcase. Not even Tanya, who assumed the worst, had been given official confirmation. This was particularly difficult given it was Tanya who'd made the first call to Crime Stoppers.

Part of Scott's promise to police had also meant he couldn't tell his son, Luke, that Khandalyce had been identified. While Luke was four years younger than Karlie, they'd been extremely close growing up. Luke had followed her path out of home, choosing to move into Connie's house when he left school and starting an apprenticeship as a glazier. Like his dad, he has a quiet, private nature about him but he hadn't shied away from defending his sister's reputation. After Karlie had left town, Luke had struck down rumours circulating Alice that she'd been involved in drugs. His loyalty to Karlie was strong and he missed her dearly.

Now, on the morning of 21 October, as Scott and Luke waited to collect Tanya from Alice Springs airport, Scott nervously wondered what was in store. Police had asked him to come to Alice Springs and he'd arrived two days earlier.

After Tanya arrived around 9 am, the three set off by car for Alice Springs police station. There was a sense of apprehension as they drove across town, with anxious silences filling the gaps between forced conversation.

For Tanya, the days waiting for the police to call with an update since she'd made the Crime Stoppers reports had been excruciating. She'd been reluctant to pester them but, as much as she wished it wasn't true, deep down she knew the girl in the suitcase was Khandalyce. Then, finally the South Australia Police had got in touch to ask her to attend a briefing at Alice Springs police station. They wouldn't tell her over the phone what the development was but she could only assume.

At the station, Major Crime detectives met them in the foyer and they walked upstairs to an empty interview room.

The investigators introduced themselves before everyone sat down. Every second that passed felt like an eternity.

Eventually, one detective began speaking. 'Your hunch was right,' he said.

'I'm sorry to tell you that the girl in South Australia has been positively identified as Khandalyce.'

Then, before Luke and Tanya could process the weight of the revelation, the detective told them there was more information he needed to share.

Since police had identified Khandalyce, they had also been trying to track down Karlie, he said. A woman's remains had been found in the Belanglo State Forest in southern New South Wales in August 2010. At the time police hadn't been able to identify her. However, five days ago, Karlie's DNA profile, generated from medical records, had been compared against Khandalyce's remains. There was a positive match.

Like Khandalyce, police believed Karlie had also been murdered and investigators were working very hard to find those responsible.

Tanya stared blankly at the detective in shock. She couldn't cry because she couldn't comprehend what was happening.

In the seat beside her, Luke had tears streaming down his face. In the past four years, he'd lost his mother to breast cancer, his Nanna Connie and now his sister and niece were dead too. Tanya's heart ached for him.

Before Scott walked into that police station, he hadn't known what had become of Karlie, though he feared the worst. 'If Khandalyce is dead, Karlie is too,' he'd said to Detective Paul Tucker nine days earlier when he'd been told about Khandalyce. Scott couldn't imagine Karlie leaving her daughter, let alone living without her. But hearing that she'd been dead for seven years, when he thought she'd been ignoring her family, and the resentment he'd felt as a result, was sickening.

Luke, Scott and Tanya were told they'd need to provide detailed statements to police over the following twenty-four hours. It would be difficult to reach so far back into their memories and process the traumatic news at the same time. The wind had been knocked out of them and their minds were foggy with grief.

As they left the police station that day, Luke, Scott and Tanya spotted news crews standing outside the courthouse.

Karlie's and Khandalyce's names and photographs would be all over the news that evening, they were sure.

It all felt too soon, as if they'd been robbed of a moment to process their loss in private before it was broadcast to the world.

Chapter 18

Daniel James Holdom paced the short distance between his bed and the sink on the opposite wall of his jail cell. A jacket, branded with Monarch Building Solutions, where he'd once worked as a labourer in Canberra, lay folded in a corner.

When Holdom had been thrown in jail a few years earlier, he'd been gaunt, a raging drug habit having reduced his towering six-foot-three frame to not much more than skin and bone. Now, at forty-one years old, he weighed more than a hundred kilograms, and his green prison jumper stretched to cover his broad, hulking shoulders and cut into his bulging neck.

With black, closely clipped hair and a nose that seemed to cover more than its fair share of his heavy-set face, he'd earned the nickname 'Shrek'. But while his appearance might have had similarities to that of the animated ogre his personality did not. Holdom could be charismatic when he wanted to be. He peppered his conversations with charm and manners and could feign genuine interest in other people.

But it was all part of the façade. Before NSW Homicide Squad detectives arrived at the jail early that morning with a warrant to search Holdom's cell, they'd already gathered information about his ex-partners, old friends, colleagues and criminal history. They had a picture of a man whose life had revolved around crime, a hoarder who left bags of his possessions at every house he stayed at, a pathological liar who used charm to deceive people, and a child abuser who was currently in Cessnock jail for sexually assaulting a child.

As police officers rummaged through his possessions, lifting up the mattress, rifling through the pockets of his jackets and sifting through documents looking for anything of evidentiary value, other inmates had looked on curiously. It was no doubt a welcome break from the dull, monotonous routine of daily prison life.

The warrant the detectives handed Holdom stated that police were investigating the murders of Karlie Pearce-Stevenson and her young daughter Khandalyce. Later, Holdom would claim it was the first he knew of their deaths. In any case, Holdom preferred to push Karlie and her daughter to the back of his mind. He'd been distracted by other demons in jail.

In the weeks prior, he'd been taking part in regular group therapy sessions that attempted to address the post-traumatic stress disorder he still grappled with following a serious car accident seven years earlier. Holdom would stay up into the early hours of the morning, scribbling into his diary about the guilt and remorse he felt for causing that crash.

Guilt. It is the guilt that is killing me, it is driving me insane, he wrote.

It was a grief no one understood.

While Holdom seemed very focused on his own suffering, police were interested in his role in the murders of the mother and child. He was an obvious suspect.

Just a month earlier, Holdom had been denied parole because he hadn't completed a sex offender's rehabilitation program and he needed to find an appropriate place to live on his release, somewhere that wouldn't encourage his descent into crime again.

Holdom had been livid. *Fuck the program, this whole thing is bullshit, I am sick of this stress,* he'd written in his diary.

The parole decision had inadvertently assisted police — with Holdom behind bars and unable to apply for parole for another twelve months, there was less risk he could tamper with evidence or interfere with witnesses.

Holdom had been sent to Cessnock jail after sexually assaulting a nine-year-old girl in a caravan in April 2013. He'd been staying at the Blue Bay Caravan Park at The Entrance with his then girlfriend, Toni Blundell, a teenager from Charnwood, one of Canberra's northern suburbs.

Toni was seventeen at the time and looked it, despite her best attempts. Long dark hair, sometimes streaked blue or pink, hung down to her hips. She'd lived in the same street as Holdom's cousin, Christine Lancaster and her husband, Dereck Dover. It was where Holdom drifted in and out of over the years, staying for a week or two at a time before up and leaving without much notice. He'd arrive unannounced at the house when he was escaping something in his life: drugs, grief or a break-up.

Toni's family, the Blundells, were friendly with Dereck and Christine and joined their weekend-long parties. Occasionally, Toni would agree to babysit Christine and

Dereck's children while they went out. This was how she met Holdom, and their relationship had blossomed.

The age gap was not lost on Dereck, who felt a strong sense of loyalty towards Holdom. They'd become mates over the years, a friendship based on sleepless weekends talking about their lives. Holdom would insist on paying for their drugs most of the time, telling Dereck he had a 'hook-up' with Centrelink that left him with large sums of cash, but he was always vague on the details.

Dereck didn't push Holdom on the subject; he respected that it was his mate's own business and besides, sometimes Dereck was the beneficiary of those welfare payments. Dereck knew about the car crash Holdom had been involved in in 2008 and felt sorry for how messed up it had left him. He felt an obligation to have Holdom's back. But when Holdom got together with Toni, Dereck thought it was a bad idea.

In any case, Dereck's loyalty was lost on Holdom, who continued to date Toni regardless.

Toni was equally defiant. No one could tell her what she could and couldn't do, and she continued to parade Holdom around the neighbourhood like he was a prized animal at a dog show. He'd follow sheepishly, keeping his head down, in what neighbours interpreted as an attempt to avoid trouble or just plain disinterest. 'How old is that guy?' bemused residents would ask the teenager's unperturbed mother.

Holdom was thirty-eight.

In the end, the relationship created a wedge between Holdom and the disapproving Dereck, forcing Holdom, in 2012, to pack up his possessions and move in with his girlfriend, where he shared the teenager's bedroom under the same roof as her father and mother.

In early 2013, the couple headed north to the Central Coast of New South Wales, where they settled at the Blue Bay Caravan Park. Holdom knew the area well, having travelled up and down the coast picking up odd jobs.

Living in the park with her mother and mother's boyfriend was a nine-year-old girl who often wandered over to Holdom's caravan to see Toni. The girls would watch movies together or play games on an iPad.

On 27 April 2013, Toni left Holdom on the Central Coast and travelled back to the ACT to see her family. Two days later, the girl, dressed in her pyjamas, strolled over to Holdom's caravan for dinner. The young girl's mother had felt comfortable enough with her daughter going to the caravan because she trusted Toni. Unfortunately, she was unaware that Toni had left for Canberra days earlier.

When the girl knocked on the door, Holdom — who later claimed he was affected by the drug ice and hadn't slept in three days — appeared and said Toni wasn't there. He invited the girl inside anyway.

The girl lay down on a bunk bed and watched *Pirates of the Caribbean* and *Hoodwinked* on a small TV while Holdom sat at the end of the bed. Slowly he inched closer until he pulled down her pyjama pants and abused her.

Two days later, the girl told her mother what had happened. As tears rolled down her cheeks, she said she'd told Holdom 'no' but he'd persisted.

'I was supposed to sleep in one bed and he was supposed to sleep in another, but he got in beside me and slept with me,' she informed her horrified mother.

When the mother's boyfriend overheard the disturbing admissions he ran to Holdom's caravan, full of rage and demanding to know what happened. Holdom lied and accused the young girl of telling stories. But petrified by the confrontation, he sprinted out of the caravan park and ran a kilometre to The Entrance Police Station. There, gasping for air and clutching the front counter, Holdom promised a constable that he hadn't touched the little girl and was being wrongly accused. In fact, Holdom claimed, she had actually told him it was an older man with grey hair that had assaulted her.

'I told her to tell her mother everything,' he said.

It was a lie he regurgitated during the police interview after his arrest, but eventually, he pleaded guilty to sexual intercourse with a child under ten.

In 2014, a judge sentenced him to four years and three months' jail with a non-parole period of two years.

He later told a psychologist that his behaviour that night was spur of the moment and stupid. 'I have a daughter of my own, a similar age,' he said. 'I'd kill someone if they did that to my daughter … I've messed that girl's life up. I would like to take it back. I feel like shit that I've now made her feel like I did as a kid. I messed her up.'

Chapter 19

On the dewy grass outside 11 Kerr Place in Charnwood, Canberra, a child's chest of drawers with flaking pink paint had been discarded. Just to the right of the front door, a video camera had been spray-painted on the wall. The mural resembled street art and seemed out of place on the suburban, brick façade. It suggested visitors should be wary, as if their every move was being watched.

The house at the end of the road with the camera painted above the door was the home of Christine and Dereck. It was where, in December 2008, he had turned up with a girl called Karlie and her daughter, Khandalyce.

Seven years later, not long after sunrise, Australian Federal Police officers knocked on the door.

Dereck and Christine had been the last people other than Holdom to see Karlie alive on the night of 14 December 2008. In separate but crucial statements they would tell police that, there had been an argument between Holdom and Karlie. Khandalyce had been left with Dereck and Christine while Holdom and Karlie took off in her Holden

Commodore. When Holdom returned the following day, around midday, he was alone.

Dereck said Holdom had a scratch on his face and had removed a blanket from the boot of Karlie's car before cleaning it. When Christine asked where Karlie was, Holdom claimed they'd had a fight and he'd dropped her off at a bus stop.

'How could she leave Khandals?' she asked.

'Sometimes she does that,' Holdom had replied. 'I'm taking her to her grandmother's,' he said.

Dereck told police that he helped Holdom trade in Karlie's car at a Canberra car dealership for an older Holden Statesman. Dereck's name was on the record of sale, which was carried out on 17 December 2008, because Holdom didn't have a licence.

Two days later, Holdom had strapped Khandalyce into a baby seat in the car and taken off for South Australia.

Christine said she never saw the toddler again, but years later — in 2011 or 2012 — the memory had played on her mind and she'd asked Holdom how he went dropping Khandalyce at her grandmother's place.

It went 'fine', he told his cousin. Khandalyce got there.

The fact that Dereck had helped get rid of Karlie's car made him a person of interest throughout the murder investigation; however, he was never charged.

There was a culture of don't ask don't tell in Charnwood, resentment towards police in general and reluctance to tell them anything. That probably had something to do with the frequent visits officers made to the suburban pocket. But it was difficult to believe that Dereck hadn't suspected something suspicious had gone on as he helped Holdom trade in Karlie's car when she was nowhere in sight.

According to Colleen's missing person's report about Karlie, it was Dereck who told Northern Territory Police back in 2009, when they contacted him about Karlie's car, that he'd dropped her at a bus stop in December 2008 and that had been the last he saw of her. But when police asked him about this in 2015 in a subsequent interview, Dereck denied ever making that comment.

While police were searching through Dereck and Christine's house on Kerr Place, there were almost identical visits being made to homes in other states and territories. Police were all looking for the same thing — evidence relating to the deaths of Karlie and Khandalyce.

Mark Ashman had once owned a DVD store at the Greenacres shopping centre in Adelaide's northwest, and was once a friend of both Holdom and Hazel. In June 2010, nearly two years after Karlie was killed, Ashman was issued a traffic infringement notice but had signed a statutory declaration saying Karlie was actually driving his Nissan Skyline at the time. At one point, according to documents later tendered in court, a new Medicare card in Karlie's name had been sent to his address. Now they turned up with a search warrant at his home on Graham Avenue in Holden Hill.

On Kerr Place, as well as number 11, police were interested in number 2, the home of the Blundell family, whose youngest daughter, Toni, had dated Holdom before he was thrown in jail for sexually assaulting a nine-year-old. Detectives had learned that Holdom had been living in the Blundell household after he'd had a fight with Dereck and before Holdom and Toni took off to the Central Coast in 2013. Holdom had a tendency to hoard and he could have left a stack of his possessions inside Toni's house somewhere.

Holdom and Toni's relationship had unravelled after Holdom was thrown in jail and, judging by Toni's social media outbursts, she despised him.

Deleting the memories I have/had of us/you, she'd written in January 2014.

In 2013: *Well Daniel hidden 2 diff phones under his car seat I found them and busted him now he saying it doesn't make up for what I did. Seems the lies and sneaking has come from both sides.*

And yet, despite the vitriol and feeling of utter hatred, Toni had never thrown out Holdom's property. Cardboard boxes and rusted car parts littered the front yard as police approached the front door. Inside the house, officers found items of interest, including Karlie's old mobile phone and Toni's diary.

Outside Toni's musky, cluttered bedroom, when she was bumming cigarettes off neighbours or threatening to punch someone's lights out, she appeared tough and rough. But the handwritten pages in her diary suggested she was like any other vulnerable teenage girl who worried about boys, friends and body image.

One entry in particular caught a detective's eye. Later tendered in court, it was dated 8 January 2013:

Well things feel diff. Daniels lied to me! Said he killed Karlie and Khandals but there still alive. It's all over Facebook … but he says their dead and he made them think she's alive but everything he says don't make sense app he killed her Dec 2008 but ppl gave her $ on her daughters Bday 2010 2011 … got a text from Hazel saying their dead and she seen pics now just waiting to see if this shirt was hers if so then she really is gone … send him a pic of her soon … he (they?) found her top and said he threw it over her no one knows who she is.

It was a startling piece of evidence that opened up other leads for police.

What were the pictures?

How did Hazel Passmore know in 2013 that Karlie was dead?

Who gave Karlie money in 2010 and 2011?

Also found at Toni's home was a mobile phone Holdom had used with Karlie's sim card after her death, and a Medicare card in the name of Karlie J Pearce-Stevenson and Khandalyce was found stashed in a drawer alongside an ANZ bank card in the name of one of Holdom's aliases, Daniel Marshall. There was also an Alice Springs Town Council public library card with Karlie's signature on the back.

**

21 October 2015, 9.09 am

Senior Constable Jason Edwards flipped open the viewer on his small handheld video camera as he walked towards the front door of 62 Ashton Road, Davoren Park.

The suburb was nestled in the northern sprawl of Adelaide, with Elizabeth to the east and MacDonald Park to the west. It was a bleak area on the city fringes, sandwiched between the wealth of the CBD and the picturesque, vineyard-lined Adelaide Hills.

Davoren Park's streets were a mix of working-class residents who lived simple orderly lives in their well cared for homes, and housing trust properties with cracked windows and rubbish strewn on the front lawns. Number 62 Ashton Road was somewhere in the middle. The large glass windows, shadowed by a brown and orange striped awning, were intact. Pieces of plywood formed a crude wheelchair ramp from the driveway to the front door. There were two Holden Commodores parked in the driveway of the red-brick house; someone was home.

Senior Constable Edwards was with a group of officers from the Major Crime Investigation Branch about to perform a search warrant on the home of Hazel Passmore. Hazel had been identified as a key person of interest in the murder investigation — not as the killer, but someone who probably knew what happened to Karlie and Khandalyce. She was with Holdom in the years before and after the mother and daughter died, and investigations so far had linked her to the fraudulent use of Karlie's bank account. Her past was about to catch up with her.

The officers walked past the steel-grey station wagon parked in the driveway and knocked on Hazel's front door. A tall gangly man opened it; he was about six foot tall, in his late thirties with a snake-like tattoo twisting around his left forearm. It was James Matheson, Hazel's boyfriend.

'Hi, how you doin'?' Detective Brevet Sergeant Amanda Bridge asked.

'Good, mate,' Matheson replied.

'We're from the police, my name's Amanda Bridge. I am a detective with the Major Crime Investigation Branch. Mate, is it all right if we just come inside, I just want you to know the camera is running,' Detective Bridge said with a nod in Senior Constable Edwards' direction. 'We're investigating a murder of Karlie Pearce-Stevenson and Khandalyce Pearce. Hazel will probably be able to talk to you about that.'

'Oooh, shit,' Matheson said, his hand still gripping the slightly ajar door.

Detective Bridge held up the general search warrant, authorising police to go through the home looking for any evidence connected to the murders.

'We suspect that there may be evidence contained within these premises, all right,' Detective Bridge said.

Matheson scratched his head. He appeared confused and shocked. 'Of a murder,' he repeated, trying to let the words sink in.

'Yes,' Detective Bridge replied.

The team of detectives walked through the front door as Hazel, still dressed in her pyjama pants, wheeled down the hallway.

The officers split up and walked into different areas of the house while a video camera remained fixed on Hazel. 'Hang on,' Matheson said, a hint of frustration in his voice. 'Who, who are these people?'

Detective Bridge answered. 'I can just let you know it's involving the murders of Khandalyce Pearce and Karlie Pearce-Stevenson.'

Hazel nodded in acknowledgement while her bewildered partner stood next to her. 'Daniel's ex,' she confirmed quietly.

A blond-haired boy about two years old, hovered around Hazel's legs, fixated on the sudden burst of activity inside his home. Hazel, Detective Bridge and Senior Constable Edwards moved into the kitchen and sat around a timber dining table covered with a bright red tablecloth. The camera focused on Hazel's face; her long brown hair was pulled back in a ponytail but a few loose strands swept across her face.

'Hazel,' Detective Bridge began. 'The reason that we're here today is in relation to the murders of Khandalyce Pearce and her mother, Karlie Pearce-Stevenson. I'm aware that you know these people … and I also know that you were in a relationship with Daniel Marshall. I suspect that you may have some knowledge or may have played a role in their murder.'

Hazel laughed nervously. 'Not at all. I can guarantee I was in hospital when he took off with her.'

From the tone of the reply, it was clear Hazel didn't view Karlie in a positive light. There was venom in the way she uttered 'her'.

'While I was in the hospital, just after I was moved to the rehab, he took off with Karlie,' Hazel reiterated. 'Karlie had come down and they'd gotten really chummy; 'cause I was in the hospital I couldn't do anything about it. But I noticed, so I told Daniel, you know, that's it, fuck off.'

Hazel's son returned and latched on to her leg. She was getting distracted and the detectives were reluctant to stop the flow of the conversation. They suggested they all move outside and sit in the unmarked police vehicle. 'You might have to tag team and get James, get Dad to have a look after him for a little while,' Senior Constable Edwards suggested over the child's cries.

Hazel handed over the toddler to her partner before he helped her into the back seat of the detective's car. The buzz of activity had drawn neighbours from their homes and out onto the street for a stickybeak.

The conversation turned to Karlie again. The detectives were keen to know how Hazel had ended up with Holdom. What Hazel didn't know was that two states away, her ex-boyfriend was about to be asked the same questions in an interview room on the Central Coast, and that her version would be compared against his to figure out where the truth lay.

Chapter 20

Following the search of his cell, Holdom made a quick call to Alex,* one of the few people he'd remained in touch with since his childhood.

In a panicked voice, Holdom whispered down the phone that he was about to be charged with two counts of murder. 'It's got Karlie's name on it,' he said.

Perhaps he was referring to documents stashed in a bag inside a kitchen cupboard at Alex's house. When Holdom, on bail for sexually assaulting a child, had been arrested again after police found drugs in his caravan, he'd asked Alex to travel to the Blue Bay Caravan Park at The Entrance to collect all the paperwork inside the caravan. He'd asked Alex to take the mobile phone too, but it couldn't be found. Whatever had been left over, apart from Holdom's clothes, had ended up in Toni Blundell's possession.

'Who's Karlie?' Alex asked.

'The girl you met at the funeral.'

---

* This person's identity has been suppressed by a court order. 'Alex' is a pseudonym.

Alex had attended Willow's and Ryan's funeral and had been introduced to Karlie. At the time, Holdom said that Karlie was staying in his motel room because she'd escaped a partner who was 'beating her'.

'Why is she stirring up trouble now?'

'I don't know,' Holdom responded. 'I've got to go.'

Then he hung up.

* * *

21 October 2015, 11 am

After sitting in the back of the detectives' car for an hour, Hazel's legs were starting to ache. Her right knee was almost pushed up against the front passenger seat.

Senior Constable Edwards and Detective Bridge could tell she was uncomfortable, and on two occasions asked if she would go down to the Elizabeth Police Station to speak with them in an interview room. Hazel agreed, but her answers kept coming, sometimes without prompting.

After telling investigators how Holdom left her on the day of her children's funeral and returned again a month later, Hazel painted a picture of a relationship that never fully recovered.

'I kept calling him a murderer and a monster and he didn't like that.'

Of course she asked where Karlie was, Hazel told police, but an evasive Holdom usually shrugged off the question. At first, he'd claimed that Karlie had gone back to her ex-boyfriend Robbie in Alice Springs, but Hazel knew that didn't stack up; Robbie was still calling her looking for Karlie. Hazel assumed Karlie was staying in the ACT and when she pushed Holdom on the subject, he said she'd actually gone to Queensland.

Her suspicions continued to fester, made worse by her deep-rooted insecurities. Over the following months, she interpreted Holdom's long absences from home, his trips back and forth between Adelaide and the ACT, as cheating. When he left the house she'd rifle through his belongings, looking for something that would validate her suspicions and confirm that she wasn't crazy.

She trawled through Holdom's internet history, text messages and phone contacts, deleting the number of any female she didn't know or anyone she felt threatened by. She rummaged through his car, furiously pushing aside bags of old clothes and fast-food wrappers, trying to beat the clock before Holdom returned home from work.

Paranoia consumed her and she was adamant Holdom was cheating on her. Every move was treated with trepidation. When he left to visit his cousins in the ACT, she was certain he was going back to see Karlie.

'What he told me was, yeah, he knew she was staying with some drug dealer fella, but I didn't believe that for a second,' Hazel said, the same contempt returning to her voice. 'I figured she was just staying with Dereck and Christine and being his bitch, you know, a bit on the side. Cos I figured that's why he was driving down there.'

When they lived together, Hazel had turned their bedroom upside down and found needles and glass pipes scattered in Holdom's cupboard — a discovery she claimed shocked her because she never knew Holdom was a drug user.

Almost on cue, a drug detection dog and its handler walked past the detectives' car towards Hazel's front door. Her eyes followed the dog as it entered the house and she was momentarily distracted; there was a marijuana plant growing in her backyard.

The detectives pushed on. Hazel started a new sentence without finishing the one before it and the interview jumped erratically from Holdom leaving Adelaide in 2008, to Hazel's rental history, to her mother's glowing first impression of Holdom. Hazel had been talking freely for two hours but it was hard to gauge when she was telling the truth and when she was lying. While the background information gathered so far would be useful, Detective Bridge eventually steered the line of questioning back to the murders.

'What I'll tell you is that Karlie's body was found in the Belanglo Forest a few years ago,' the detective said.

'Where's Belanglo?' Hazel asked.

'New South Wales,' Detective Bridge answered. 'And Khandalyce was the body in the suitcase.'

'Oh, I remember having a conversation about that,' Hazel offered.

Intrigued, Detective Bridge asked her to go on.

'I seen the pictures and the clothing. There's two pieces of clothing that really stood out in my mind that I seen when they posted it. I remember saying to Jimmy [James]: "Jeez, that looks like …" Then he goes: "Oh, you should probably say something." "I was like, "No".' Hazel laughed nervously.

'What pieces of clothing?' Detective Bridge asked.

'Um, a little black dress with sparkles on it and the, the coat, because Lauryn had exactly the same one that we used to dress them up. Lauryn had a purple one and I can't remember what colour hers was, its either pink or white. But they both had the same coat, and yeah, it just looked really familiar.'

Hazel thought she'd seen Khandalyce wearing a black tutu, she added, similar to the one found in the suitcase.

The information rang alarm bells and provided a potential link between Khandalyce's remains and Holdom's inner circle. Detectives were on the right track but they remained non-committal, almost blasé, so as not to alert Hazel the detectives were on to something.

It was an uncomfortable topic to address but the detectives had to ask Hazel about her sexual history with Holdom. They knew he had a sexual interest in children, and other women he'd been with had detailed his unusual fantasies. If Hazel had been with Holdom for several years she more than likely knew about it.

Hesitant initially, Hazel relaxed and admitted how she would write out erotic stories at Holdom's request before they had sex. It was how he got aroused, she said, but sometimes the topics waded into depraved territory — sex involving children. She acted as if the topic disgusted her, but Hazel had been caught with child exploitation material during a police raid on her home in Tin Can Bay in 2006 (much later, in 2017, she was charged and convicted). There had been three posters hanging in her room — cartoons of children being sexually abused by other children while their mothers watched on.

At the time Hazel had shrugged off the perversion and claimed a friend gave them to her, but she was eventually placed on a six-month good behaviour bond for the possession of child exploitation material.

In her unrelenting search for a sign that Holdom was having an affair, Hazel had monitored his computer activity and found he was also looking up pornography involving young girls around 2009. Proudly, Hazel claimed she'd used the IT skills she'd learned at TAFE to put a program on their computer that secretly recorded the websites Holdom visited.

'He's addicted to porn,' she said matter-of-factly.

The police were dealing with the death of a child and the information Hazel had provided confirmed Holdom had a sexual interest in children. It was a link that needed to be explored further.

'What I would like to ask you is, you talked before about some things you found, sex sites, that were on the computers,' Detective Bridge continued. 'Were there any pictures like that on those computers?'

'Yeah,' Hazel replied. 'There was, um, like thousands of downloads of young girls. I can guarantee you some of them were underage and some of them just looked underage.'

Casually, without breaking from the flow of the conversation, Detective Bridge asked if there were any photos of Karlie or Khandalyce.

'Yes,' Hazel said quietly. There was a pause. Hazel wasn't going to give the information up willingly.

'What were they?' Detective Bridge pressed.

'Well, one she's laying half-naked on her back with an alcohol bottle, and he reckons, they were fucking around in the thing … 'Cause I asked, "What's the go with the photo," you know? And he tried to first say it wasn't Karlie. I was like, there's no way that person is not Karlie. Karlie's so skinny and you just know her straightaway. He just reckoned, you know, that was ages ago, out, you know … he reckoned that photo was taken in Alice Springs. But, yeah, I don't think so.'

Detective Bridge couldn't believe what she was hearing and continued on carefully. 'Describe what the picture looked like.'

'Er, a girl laying on her back,' Hazel said, 'and there was an alcohol bottle between her legs. That's all I can remember.'

Hazel, recalling the photo, said to the police that Karlie's eyes were closed, she was wearing a T-shirt, lying next to a big tree or a log, and her face was turned away or covered by a branch. There was no red dirt, so Hazel doubted the photograph was taken anywhere in Alice Springs.

While she was hazy on the details about exactly what Karlie was wearing, the image of the bottle was imprinted in her memory; it was the most shocking part of the photo.

The photo was on a memory card along with another photograph of Khandalyce sleeping in a car seat, she said.

The description Hazel had provided, particularly the reference to the log and Karlie in a T-shirt, was chillingly similar to the setting in which Karlie's remains had been found.

Detective Bridge asked what else Holdom said when asked about the photo.

Hazel began to stutter and her sentences were broken, as though she couldn't decide how to answer. Holdom claimed he and Karlie had been 'mucking around' Hazel said, and she didn't press it any further because she figured Karlie was posing for him.

Detective Bridge suspected Hazel knew more than she was letting on. At first Hazel had said the photo was on a computer, then that it was on a sim card and then an SD card. Maybe Hazel was confused, maybe she was trying to cover her tracks, but she was not coming across as a particularly reliable witness.

Detective Bridge asked what happened to the SD card.

'He had them all, as far as I know he had them all, last I knew,' Hazel said, before denying she ever copied the images.

The topic changed suddenly and Detective Bridge asked Hazel if she and Holdom, while travelling around Australia, had ever taken any towels or mementoes from the motels they stayed in. Police were still trying to track down the origin of clothing and a towel found in the suitcase with Khandalyce's bones. They had contacted dozens of motels around South Australia looking for towels with the same batch number. If they could ascertain a link between Holdom and the towel, they might be able to narrow down the search to the motels he'd stayed in.

Hazel paused to think. They might have, she said. She remembered taking one home from the hospital accidentally.

A few minutes later, another detective brought out a green-coloured towel found in a bedroom at the rear of Hazel's house. There had originally been two of the same towel, she said. She and Daniel had taken them from a hotel they'd stayed in, possibly at Victor Harbor.

The towel was placed in a brown evidence bag marked ARD11.

Detective Bridge began to wrap up the interview and asked Hazel to contact her if she thought of any other relevant information. There was more to the story and Hazel might have been withholding information, either motivated by self-interest or because she was embarrassed. Many of her answers had painted Holdom in an extremely negative light — a disgusting person, a man of no morals, a boyfriend she couldn't shake — while putting herself on the moral high ground. Hazel had spent several years in a relationship with Holdom; it was difficult to believe she hadn't gleaned more information about the fate of Karlie and Khandalyce during that time.

'So what will happen from here is, we'll finish up today and I'll get back in touch with you at some point,' Detective Bridge said.

At 1:05 pm, Senior Constable Edwards turned off the camera recording the interview. There was a mountain of information to sift through following the interview but the priority was finding the photographs of Karlie.

Chapter 21

21 October 2015, 11 am

Editors and news directors were discussing the stories of the morning, figuring out a rough plan of what would go where in the next day's edition of the *Sydney Morning Herald* newspaper.

It was a few minutes past 11 am and most journalists in the Pyrmont newsroom had arrived in the office. The online desk was winding down after the morning rush and TVs scattered around the open-plan office provided subtle background noise.

Politics dominated the morning news list and there was an arrest for a gangland murder in Sydney overnight, but page one — the coveted spot every journalist vied for — was still up for grabs. Crime editor Nick Ralston was confident he had a contender.

Having covered police rounds for six years, Ralston had reported on some of Sydney's biggest crimes, including the case of Angel — the woman's skeleton found in Belanglo State Forest in August 2010. Earlier that morning, he'd received a tip-off about an explosive story that was going to break later in the day. The caller couldn't say too much, but suggested it would be in Ralston's best interests if he sent a reporter out to the State Crime Command in Parramatta that afternoon. The only hint the tipster gave was that the press conference would reveal links between two high-profile cases.

The intrigue had everyone guessing, and journalists on Ralston's team gathered around his corner desk to speculate about what the cases could be. With 700-odd unsolved homicides in New South Wales, the combination was anyone's guess. Missing toddler William Tyrrell? The unsolved murder of IT worker Prabha Kumar in Parramatta? The baby in the suitcase in South Australia?

Unbeknown to the media, the movements of police throughout that morning had been planned meticulously across four jurisdictions; search warrants had been rolled out simultaneously to avoid anyone tipping off anyone else.

Even the timing of the press conference was methodical. The heads of the South Australia Major Crime Investigation Branch and NSW Homicide Squad would address the media in their respective states at exactly the same time. Police needed time to reach some of the addresses they had to search, and putting the news out too early could force witnesses to destroy evidence or flee.

For the past week the operation had been under tight wraps. Specific detectives were updated on a need-to-know basis, and a media officer was briefed forty-eight hours prior, as late in the game as possible to ensure the developing breakthrough was kept quiet.

At 11:20 am, a media alert was issued to newsrooms across the state, confirming Ralston's tip.

'Police in New South Wales and South Australia will announce a recent breakthrough linking two suspected murder investigations.

'NSW Police Force Homicide Squad Commander, Detective Superintendent Mick Willing, and South Australia Police Head of Major Crime, Detective Superintendent Des Bray, will conduct simultaneous media conferences to announce an investigative link between two major investigations.

'No further information is available at this time.'

***

21 October 2015, 1 pm

At State Crime Command, special constables directed journalists to the briefing room in time for the 1:30 pm press conference. Cameramen set up at the back of the room while reporters discussed the mind-boggling breakthrough in hushed tones.

The *Daily Telegraph* had broken the news online about an hour before the press conference was due to start. Every journalist knew the two cases at the centre of the announcement were the bones found in Belanglo in August 2010, and the girl found in the suitcase in July 2015. The New South Wales investigation had been named Strike Force Malaya, replacing Strike Force Hixson, which had been the investigation into the unidentified remains known as Angel.

Reporters tried to untangle the logistics by discussing the bare facts: a baby stuffed in a suitcase over 1100 kilometres away from her mother in a different state, and found five years apart.

Upstairs in the belly of State Crime Command, Detective Superintendent Michael Willing was preparing for what he would say to the waiting media contingent. The entry to the Homicide Squad office was a narrow hallway, plastered with newspaper clippings of the elite team's most significant arrests over decades. Black and white photos showed old-school detectives frog-marching infamous underworld identities Arthur 'Neddy' Smith and Billy Munday to the back of paddy wagons.

Down the hall of fame, past the lunchroom and to the left, Superintendent Willing was seated behind his desk, the door to his neat office closed. It had become a habit for him to spend a few minutes by himself before every press conference. He'd go over the main messages in his head and the potentially prickly questions he'd field from journalists. He swore by these moments of solitude as a means of putting him in the right mindset, and on this day he needed it.

Willing had spent the morning with Detective Inspector Jason Dickinson — in charge of the on-call team handling New South Wales' share of the investigation — as updates from the search warrants unfolding around the country streamed in. For the past seven days, the team had been discreetly tracking down Holdom's former associates and ex-partners to get a sense of who their main suspect was. His roots spread from the central west to the Hunter region to Sydney's southwest and interstate.

A woman from the New South Wales Southern Highlands, who had dated Holdom many years before, provided an insight into his warped sexual fantasies; another reported finding disturbing photographs in October 2010 of a young girl with blood dripping down her legs. Police would never find evidence of those photographs.

The depravity of the crime would not be detailed at the press conference. The aim was to reveal the link between the two cases, identify the victims, and push the faces of the mother and child out into the public eye in the hope of generating more information about their last days alive.

Willing and Dickinson caught the lift down to the mezzanine level, and then took the escalator to the lobby. Detective Willing viewed Dickinson as one of his brightest inspectors — a brilliant detective and a quiet achiever with a sharp mind, who was touted for big things in the police force. Dickinson had earned a reputation for being a bit gruff; perhaps it was his complete lack of interest in building a profile for himself. To those closest to him, it was a humility; he simply wanted to solve murders without the fanfare.

'We right to go?' Detective Willing asked the curious media pack. He could sense the anticipation in the room. This was a big story and everyone knew it, but five years as the head of the NSW Homicide Squad had taught him to mask his nerves with confidence. He'd earned a reputation as an ambitious detective who'd cut his teeth as a cop in the bush in Dubbo, before slowly ascending to head the Homicide Squad in a high-profile and high-pressure role. He'd watched his teams crack protracted and complex investigations over the years, but this one was turning out to be one of the most perplexing and rapidly moving cases he'd ever worked on.

The questions came in thick and fast and Willing sounded as mystified as the reporters at one point.

'It's absolutely baffling,' he said, staring down the barrel of the camera. 'Here we have a young mum and a little girl who decide to leave the Northern Territory for whatever reason ... and travel around Australia, and then their remains are discovered years later. It's a complete mystery to us.'

A reporter asked whether Khandalyce's father was a suspect.

'I can say the family are not involved,' he replied firmly.

***

In Adelaide, at the South Australia Police headquarters on Angas Street, Detective Des Bray was fielding questions from another camp of reporters.

'I can tell you in recent days we had the breakthrough and a considerable amount of work has been done across the country by a variety of people,' he said, regularly glancing between the papers in his hand and over the row of microphones. 'I can tell you it's caller 1267 and 1271 that provided the crucial breakthrough.'

Before journalists scrambled to file for their respective outlets, media officers in both states handed out a statement from the family of Khandalyce and Karlie.

> The families of Karlie and Khandalyce are grateful to the police, the community and media and everyone who has assisted or provided information in this investigation.
>
> As you would expect our family is devastated by this news of the deaths of Karlie and Khandalyce and we are trying to deal with the grief.
>
> We understand that this case has created considerable interest across the country but at this time we ask that you respect our privacy to allow us to grieve.
>
> Thank you.

Their appeal for privacy seemed to resonate with the tight-knit community in Alice Springs. Apart from the odd comment from an old school friend or sporting coach, there was little information about Karlie's and Khandalyce's backgrounds getting out of Alice Springs, despite the intense media attention.

The fact Scott knew that Khandalyce had been identified several days earlier was the cause of some angst in the family. He'd stuck to his promise to police that he wouldn't tell a soul, leaving the rest of Karlie's family none the wiser until the story broke on the afternoon of 21 October 2015.

Colleen Povey with her young daughter Karlie Jade Pearce-Stevenson. Colleen moved to Alice Springs when she was pregnant and gave birth to Karlie on 7 August 1988. She later met husband Scott Povey and the pair had a son together in 1992, Karlie's younger brother, Luke. *(Scott Povey)*

Karlie, aged four or five, sitting on the kitchen bench of the family home in Braitling in Alice Spring's northern suburbs. She was just about to help her stepfather, Scott, cut his hair when this photograph was taken. *(Scott Povey)*

Police released this photograph to the media on 21 October 2015 when it was first revealed the remains found in Belanglo State Forest in August 2010 were of Karlie. The image became synonymous with the case.
(Scott Povey)

Karlie Pearce-Stevenson, twenty, with daughter, Khandalyce, two. This photograph was taken by Karlie's aunty in Port Augusta in November 2008. Karlie stopped by to visit her family after leaving Alice Springs with Khandalyce and Daniel Holdom.

The entry to Belanglo State Forest in New South Wales's Southern Highlands. The forest gained notoriety as serial killer Ivan Milat's dumping ground. The bodies of seven backpackers had been found in the area in the late 1980s and early 1990s. *(Fairfax)*

Forensic police taped off an area near the Red Arm Creek Firetrail after trail bike riders found human bones on 29 August 2010. There was early speculation that the remains could have belonged to Ivan Milat's eighth victim. He was ruled out when forensic testing suggested the body had been left there after Milat went to jail. *(Fairfax)*

Dashcam footage on the Karoonda Highway near Wynarka, in South Australia's Murray Mallee region, captures a grey suitcase (right of frame) on the side of the highway in late May 2015. *(SA Police)*

Major Crime Investigation Branch detectives at the crime scene on the Karoonda Highway in July 2015. Three mates driving to Adelaide had pulled over at the remote spot and found the suitcase with children's bones and clothes. The skull was strapped with masking tape. *(Newspix)*

South Australia Police's Major Crime Investigation Branch boss Detective Superintendent Des Bray. At a press conference in Adelaide on 26 July 2015, police dressed a small mannequin in a blonde wig and one of the dresses found in the suitcase. Forensic odontology estimated the victim's age at death was between 1.2 and 4.8 years. *(Newspix)*

A photograph of the suitcase and two items found inside, a Cotton On black tutu dress and a pink slipper with a butterfly motif. About thirty items, mostly clothing, were found with the remains.
(SA Police)

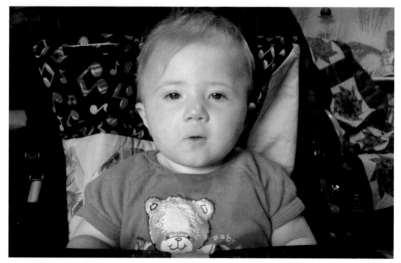

In October 2015, Scott Povey's sister, Sue, found this photograph of Khandalyce sitting in a stroller with a blanket behind her head. The blanket's colourful music notes matched the material of a quilt found in the suitcase. The blanket had been made by Scott's mother and given to Khandalyce in 2007. *(Scott Povey)*

New South Wales Homicide Squad Detective Inspector Jason Dickinson holds up photographs of Karlie Pearce-Stevenson and Khandalyce at a press conference in Sydney on 21 October 2015. It was the first time the major breakthrough in the two cases and identities of the victims were revealed. *(AAP)*

On 21 October 2015, South Australia Police raided the Davoren Park home of Hazel Passmore. Passmore was in a relationship with Daniel Holdom up until early 2012. Holdom had caused a car crash in September 2008 that killed two of Hazel's children and left her disabled. *(AAP)*

Prison guards escort Holdom, then forty-four, into the back of a prison truck at the New South Wales Supreme Court. On 30 November 2018, he was sentenced to two terms of life imprisonment for the murders. *(Fairfax)*

New South Wales Homicide Squad commander Detective Superintendent Scott Cook (centre) and officer in charge Detective Sergeant Darryn Gunn (left) address the media after Holdom's sentencing in November 2018. Cook acknowledged the suffering of Karlie and Khandalyce's family, who stood with him. Karlie's aunty, Raylene Bell, is on the far right. *(AAP)*

Karlie and Khandalyce's family and friends carry their coffin from the Desert Life Church in Alice Springs at their funeral on 11 December 2015. The pallbearers included: (left, front to back) Karlie's best friend, Jade Randle, Christie Bell (cousin), Andrew Hill (Karlie's ex-boyfriend); (right, front to back) Karlie's cousins, Jordy Bell, Samantha Harris and Adam Harris. *(Newspix)*

Chapter 22

'Can you tell me how it is you know Karlie Jade Pearce-Stevenson?'

Detective Sergeant Darryn Gunn sat opposite Holdom in a small interview room at Cessnock Police Station. They were seated at either end of a table with barely a metre between them. A video camera recorded the conversation from one end of the windowless room.

Over the course of Detective Gunn's twenty-seven-year career, he couldn't count on two hands how many homicides he'd investigated. Despite the mystique and prowess associated with working in the NSW Homicide Squad, it was a job he carried out without ego or fanfare. His work was serious and at times grim, but he was personable. He organised the social committee events for his colleagues, who knew him as a down-to-earth bloke who worked hard but knew how to have a good time.

The task of interviewing Holdom fell to Gunn, who was running New South Wales' portion of the investigation. Ever since police had identified the skeleton found in

Belanglo State Forest as Karlie Pearce-Stevenson, Gunn had spent every day learning everything he could about her, Khandalyce and Holdom. He had the best knowledge of the suspect and was best placed to interview him.

Detective Brevet Sergeant Rod Huppatz from the Major Crime Investigation Branch in South Australia had flown up to New South Wales to take part in the interview. The detectives had different areas they wanted to focus on, and had discussed their individual strategies before walking into the room.

'Um, I met her in Alice Springs as a friend and then was in a relationship with her for about eight weeks,' Holdom told the detective within the first few minutes of the interview. 'Um, yeah, that's it. Oh, we had a fight at me cousin's house 'cause she owed me cousin board. She left her cards with us as payment, she took off. Ah, she left Khandals with us for about a week.'

It was a surprisingly frank answer to receive early in an interview; it felt like Holdom was pre-empting the questions and explanations police were looking for.

'Is there anything you can tell me about your relationship with Karlie?' Detective Gunn asked.

'It's just, yeah, I don't know what you'd call it, just was a way of escaping, I think, for me,' Holdom answered. 'Just like, yeah, after the accident, didn't know what to do. I was sort of scared, sort of thing. She was sort of there to comfort me.'

Holdom began to explain how he first came to meet Karlie, but he was delving into dangerous, possibly self-incriminating territory. Detective Gunn warned him that whatever he said about criminal activity could be used against him so he should be mindful. Holdom was a man with a long and documented history of lying to get himself out of tight spaces. He'd forged a criminal career committing unsophisticated frauds and ripping people off; anything he said during the interview would have to be verified and compared against the statements of others. Problem was, there were a lot of people who had a lot to lose by telling the truth.

The tone of the interview was set with general questions about how Holdom ended up in Alice Springs, his work, history with drugs, and his relationship with Hazel. Holdom mentioned how he and Hazel had met Karlie and her then boyfriend, Robbie, in Alice Springs in 2007 and how the couples would hang out together at Holdom's house, where he sold drugs, ran a car-detailing business and brought up three kids. He appeared reasonably comfortable with his answers and attempted to seem helpful, like he had nothing to hide.

But his shoulders tensed as the interview turned to the fatal car accident in 2008. It was clear Holdom was uncomfortable.

'We've got to be careful here a bit. I think potentially this is a very traumatic area to talk about,' Detective Huppatz said cautiously.

Detective Gunn offered Holdom a break and a chance to have some water but Holdom shook his head; he wanted to push through it and get the subject over with.

'I'll go through this part first and then that way we don't come back to it, sort of thing,' he mumbled.

'Okay,' Detective Huppatz continued. 'So did Hazel get to Alice Springs Hospital or was she taken straight to Adelaide?'

'I gave her first aid at the scene,' Holdom replied, his voice lowered and eyes shifting between the tabletop and the detective's stare. Holdom then gave an account of the aftermath of the accident.

Two days after the accident, Holdom said, a friend picked him and Lauryn up from the hospital in Alice Springs and they drove straight down to Adelaide to be by Hazel's bedside.

'What condition were you in when you were driven down?' Detective Huppatz asked.

'Um, wasn't the greatest,' Holdom answered. 'Still had glass in me head. I got to Adelaide Hospital expecting to see me partner and I was refused entry into the intensive care unit because of the blood and I had a broken thumb, collarbone, so they said you can't go … They made me get medical treatment so that I could see me partner.'

Holdom stayed in a motel on Dequetteville Terrace at Kent Town, not far from the Royal Adelaide Hospital. Two rooms were booked as Hazel's sister, Amanda Evans, and her partner Chris Evans rushed to the city to give their support when news of the crash reached them.

While Hazel was in a coma, Holdom said he received news that their house back in Alice Springs had been broken into and damaged by fire. Leaving Lauryn in the care of Amanda at the motel, Holdom claimed he drove back up to Alice Springs to assess the damage, before grabbing some clothes and returning to Adelaide.

By the time he arrived, he said, Hazel was coming out of the coma. She woke to the devastating news that two of her children had been killed in the crash, a grave loss she blamed on Holdom.

'I think it was about a month later, I don't know, sometime during when Hazel was in Hampstead that I went back up, packed up half our, like all the stuff I could fit, met up with Karlie and she came back down with us,' Holdom said.

The detectives were 563 questions in and they'd at last reached the topic they were most interested in — Karlie. They wanted to hear Holdom's version of events of how Karlie had come into the picture in Adelaide.

'Why did she come back with you?' Detective Huppatz queried.

Holdom said, ''Cause I was a mess, it was like another support thing, and support sort of led to, like a relationship sort of thing. I wasn't coping on me own 'cause of Hazel and sort of blaming me about the accident.'

'Were Hazel and Karlie good friends in Alice Springs?' Detective Huppatz asked.

'They were, yes,' Holdom replied.

'So she came back as you said, sort of like a support person for you, is that right?'

'Yeah,' Holdom said.

Investigators had come into the interview with a rough idea of when Karlie had left her hometown. They'd traced her movements in late 2008 by tracking interactions she'd had with police on the roads, and through statements from the close friends who last saw her.

Police believed Karlie and Holdom had travelled from Alice Springs to Adelaide twice. The first time was on 25 October, when Karlie had received a speeding ticket on the Port Wakefield Road, the main thoroughfare into Adelaide. That day, Karlie had left Alice Springs with Khandalyce in the back seat of her Holden Commodore. Holdom claimed he'd travelled to Adelaide with Chris in his car, the two cars forming a convoy.

The second time was when Karlie had left Alice Springs on around 10 November. On this occasion, she'd stopped in to her mother's place to say goodbye.

Once they'd reached Adelaide, Holdom had returned to the hotel where Hazel's sister Amanda was still staying. Karlie and Holdom stayed at the hotel for around two weeks, until the day after Willow's and Ryan's funeral. Then, he said he left Adelaide with Karlie and Khandalyce, claiming that Hazel's family were sending him threatening text messages, saying he'd 'pay' for what he did. They drove to the ACT, where they spent several days at his aunt's house in Belconnen. But Holdom claimed that his aunt's self-centred attitude drove him nuts, so they left and went to stay with his cousin Christine Lancaster and her husband Dereck Dover.

Holdom said they were all immersed in a daily cycle of drug abuse with Holdom using ice, ecstasy pills and cannabis to pay his way in terms of board and the little food he ate.

Tensions began to flare between Karlie and Christine. The animosity was sparked by a few factors, Holdom said — Karlie falling behind with her board and taking Christine to task on her attitude and for not looking after her children better.

On 14 December 2008, the tensions boiled over and ended in a heated argument between Karlie, Dereck and Christine. Exactly what happened next was unclear, and varied depending on who police spoke to.

'Karlie went outside and sat on the back step,' Holdom said, following her fight with Christine and Dereck. 'I said, "What's going on?" She goes, "They want me to leave." So it's like, shit, what do we do?' Holdom said he found Karlie cheap accommodation and paid for it a week in advance. 'I brought Khandals back because she wasn't going to look after Khandals in her state, like, drugged up. I left her some pills and some ice and whatever else she wanted.'

It was a subtle smear on Karlie, particularly on her responsibility as a mother, to justify why Holdom ended up alone with her daughter.

The detectives were not going to accept his version without details — the motel name, the address, how much it cost, whose name it was booked under, whether it was paid in cash and if he got a receipt.

Holdom stumbled over his answers: it was a big motel, he said, on Northbourne Avenue, a major thoroughfare that connected Canberra's city centre with the northern suburbs.

'There'd be a paper trail somewhere there for that,' Holdom said of the $560 he supposedly stumped up for Karlie's accommodation.

Detective Gunn pressed him further. 'So you got a receipt for that motel?'

Yes, Holdom confirmed.

The detectives took notes of these details as they weaved in and out of different topics, jumping from one point of interest to another, and revisiting Holdom's answers in search for inconsistencies. They knew that it's harder to remember a lie than the truth.

After dropping Karlie at the motel and walking her to her room, Holdom said he returned to his cousin's house where he bathed and fed Khandalyce before putting her to bed.

'What did Karlie think about you leaving the motel with Khandals?' Detective Gunn asked.

'Oh, she was happy,' Holdom said confidently. 'I don't think she really wanted to deal with [her], 'cause she couldn't … I don't think she could control her properly, if that makes sense. Like she could, but she frustrated her. So it was just easier if I took her, and I knew how to look after kids and that, done it all me life, so …'

This contradicted information from Karlie's family that she was reluctant to go anywhere without her daughter.

Holdom said Karlie stayed in the motel for a week and a half before he left Canberra and headed back to Adelaide to be with Hazel. At least, that was Holdom's first version of events. He would go on to contradict that several times during the course of the interview, which only confirmed to police that Holdom was their key suspect.

* * *

21 October 2015, 2 pm

Raylene Bell was driving home from work at Naracoorte Hospital when her mobile phone started to ring constantly. She was strict when it came to talking on the phone while driving and her husband, Nick Bell, knew that. But when he kept ringing, she sensed the urgency and pulled over in the rain to take his call.

'What's the matter, Nick?' Ray asked as soon as she answered the phone.

Nick had just finished a call to their daughter, who'd told him to check the news urgently. He'd pulled up a web browser on his work desktop computer and punched in a news site address. The faces of his missing niece and her daughter stared back at him. It seemed that police had finally identified the remains of the child in the suitcase found in South Australia, as well as a young woman found murdered in New South Wales' Belanglo State Forest. The news was horrifying: they were Karlie and Khandalyce.

In the photo, Karlie and Khandalyce were cheek to cheek, smiling. It was the photo that had been taken at Karlie's grandmother's house in Port Augusta in South Australia many years earlier.

'It's Karlie and Khandals,' Nick said to Ray. 'They've found them.'

Ray was home within ten minutes and found Nick waiting for her in the front yard. She wasn't sure what to feel — confusion, anger, loss and a deep sense of sadness. After all these years trying to find the girls, from cold-calling schools to see if Khandalyce was enrolled, to door-knocking a house that Karlie's car was registered to, and spending hours trawling social media for anyone who resembled the mother and child, they'd been dead all along.

'We never thought they were dead, never,' Ray recalled later.

Nick agreed. 'Never crossed our minds.'

Within hours, family members — including Ray and Nick — had reporters camped outside their homes, at their work, calling their mobiles constantly and filling their Facebook inboxes with requests for interviews. The constant attention was unlike anything they had ever experienced or wanted.

Chapter 23

'So you dropped Khandals at the motel with Karlie?'

Detectives Huppatz and Gunn had been interviewing Holdom for almost three hours and they were coming to the finer details of Khandalyce's last days alive. South Australia Police had done a lot of the heavy lifting in the early stages of the investigation, when the suitcase with Khandalyce's bones turned up on their doorstep. Naturally, Detective Huppatz was interested in finding out what had happened to Khandalyce and whether she'd been killed in their jurisdiction.

He believed Karlie had been killed in December 2008, and that her daughter was murdered not long after, but exactly where was unknown. Holdom's version of events did not fit this theory but the detective listened patiently to his explanations, careful not to give anything away with his body language or follow-up questions.

At fifty-three years old, Huppatz had moved into the Major Crime Investigation Branch relatively late in his career. Since joining the team in 2008 he'd worked on twenty murder cases and, like most of his colleagues, he found the deaths of children the most challenging to investigate. It was easy for his mind to wander after he clocked off and returned home to his wife. He thought about the young victims, the cases that remained unsolved for decades and the families that struggled with unanswered questions.

Perhaps he'd been destined for serious crime investigation from a young age. According to the *Police Journal*, his mother had a childhood photograph of Huppatz at age four standing at Glenelg Beach on Australia Day in 1966, the day South Australia's most baffling and high-profile crime was carried out: the abduction of the three Beaumont children. He was too young to realise it but he would go on to follow in the footsteps of those police officers that swarmed the busy beach that day looking for answers for panicked families.

Detective Huppatz leaned back in his chair and rubbed his hand over his thick grey moustache. One of the most effective tools in an interview room is the pregnant pause: ask a question, maintain eye contact, be quiet and wait. The silence is uncomfortable, especially for a person with something to hide.

Holdom filled the protracted silences with words — lengthy, conflicting explanations about why he had Karlie's bank cards, why he traded in her car and when he saw her last. There was a self-serving tone to his answers. When asked what Karlie's aspirations were, Holdom said they were to settle down with him. He constantly found a way to bring the conversation back to the car crash in 2008, his toxic relationship with Hazel, or the problems he had with drug abuse. He painted himself as a victim, which appeared to be his way of rationalising his life decisions.

Holdom feigned a willingness to do whatever he could to assist police in catching the killer. The detectives could tell he was lying and trying to hide something, based on the varying versions he was providing, but at times he was oddly convincing.

Detective Huppatz turned the interview to 15 December 2008, when Holdom claimed he dropped Karlie at a motel in Canberra. He wanted to know why Holdom got rid of her car so quickly after she was last seen.

Yes, Holdom admitted, he had left the motel in Karlie's car, but she'd agreed to it as a way of paying the $500 debt back to Christine and Dereck. She'd even signed the transfer papers Dereck took into Belconnen Cheaper Cars two days later to trade the car in for something else, he said.

Detective Huppatz pulled out a copy of the dealer's notice detailing the vehicle trade-in on 17 December 2008. The document showed Karlie's 1996 Holden Commodore Executive Wagon was traded in for a Holden VQ Statesman sedan plus $50 cash. For some reason, Karlie's later model car was worth less than the earlier model Statesman Holdom ended up with.

When the detectives brought this up, Holdom appeared perplexed and agreed it didn't make sense. However, he pointed out — possibly in an attempt to direct the suspicion elsewhere — that Dereck had carried out the trade. He used to work as a mechanic, he knew the industry well and Holdom didn't have a licence at the time; essentially Dereck had taken care of it.

It was an unlikely story that Karlie would agree to leave both her car and her bank card with Holdom while she stayed on her own in Canberra. At first, Holdom said Karlie's car was in bad shape and wouldn't have got him to Adelaide. Later in the interview he said the car was in schmick condition with new tyres and not a spot of rust on it.

Either way, for one reason or another, Holdom had gotten rid of Karlie's car as quickly as he could after she left Charnwood, and the detectives could only assume there was something in that car that Holdom or Dereck didn't want people to see.

Holdom told police that, along with leaving him her car, Karlie gave him her bank card to help pay back the debt she owed him for drugs.

'I said, "You owe me money," so she said take the card and whenever money goes in there, take it off the thing,' Holdom explained. 'So I took it off the debt.'

Detective Huppatz queried what that meant for a single mother left in a city on her own, with no family and no money.

'So she had enough to get by. Like I said, I fucked up by not going back, and yeah, I sent her card back to her,' Holdom replied.

He sent the card in the mail back to his cousin's house in Charnwood a few months later, he said, because he assumed Karlie was still in Canberra.

Initially, when the detectives asked Holdom when he'd last seen Karlie alive, he claimed it was in December 2008. Holdom decided he was going back to Adelaide for Christmas to see Lauryn so he drove over to the motel Karlie was staying at and dropped Khandalyce off. Promising to return, he set off to South Australia, passing through Wagga Wagga on his way. But when he arrived at Hazel's home he realised he'd made a mistake; he wanted to give their relationship another go. He informed Karlie of his decision and she wasn't happy, but he never saw her again.

However, over the course of the interview, Holdom contradicted this version several times: Karlie actually turned up in Adelaide in early 2009; she stayed for a couple of months; she stayed for a year; she moved to Queensland; she ran off with a drug dealer in Coffs Harbour.

His lies grew in desperation as the interview went on. The detectives carefully noted the conflicting information until eventually calling him out — why were his claims not stacking up?

Well, Holdom began cautiously, he'd actually continued seeing Karlie in Adelaide in 2009 but he didn't want Hazel to find out.

'I was cheating,' he offered sheepishly. He asked the detectives if they'd tell Hazel; he didn't want to lose access to Lauryn, who he claimed was his daughter.

'Mate, it's none of her business,' Detective Gunn reassured him.

That prompted Holdom to change his story: Karlie and Khandalyce arrived in Adelaide on a bus from Canberra a few days after New Year's Day in 2009. They stayed at a motel and Holdom went to visit. He and Karlie were intimate, went shopping, spent a few hours together and he left again. Karlie 'hung around for about a couple of months' in Adelaide, but later in the interview Holdom extended that time period to about a year.

It was hard to keep up with Holdom's story — it changed by the hour and Detective Huppatz was deeply suspicious. 'You can see it looks bad that she's dead and Khandals is dead too,' he said. 'It looks bad that she's dead and you're using — and I suspect she died around that time — that you're using her card in Adelaide. And her car's been sold too.' They were the strongest words the detective had used yet to indicate their suspicions.

From that point, Holdom knew where he stood. 'I had nothing to do with her death, like, I don't know how I'll prove that to youse but ...' Holdom said. 'I was already going through me own trauma, like with losing me kids, why am I going to kill someone else?'

Chapter 24

Still in the interview room with Daniel Holdom, Detective Huppatz scanned a list of numbers and figures in front of him. He was looking for one entry in particular.

Long before the interviewing at Cessnock Police Station had begun, he'd gained access to the bank records of three key people — Holdom, Karlie and Hazel. There were striking correlations between some of the transactions that seemed to place the three people in the same locations at the same time after Karlie had died.

He studied the list of transactions from Karlie's Australian Central Credit Union account between November 2008 and 2015, when it was closed after a long period of inactivity. It was almost certain that Karlie had died in December 2008, but her bank account was accessed up until 2012.

Her personal bank card was used and, in June 2010, someone had physically been into the credit union pretending to be Karlie to get access to her account and update her details. Detectives had accessed branch records in Elizabeth and discovered a woman in a wheelchair, accompanied by a man who looked a lot like Holdom, went into the branch purporting to be Karlie.

They'd succeeded. Along with getting a new bank card to access Karlie's account, they'd changed the address details on file so any mail would be sent to the Adelaide home where Hazel and Holdom were living at the time. The same address was placed on Karlie's Centrelink and Medicare file.

Four years after Karlie died, a total of $71,770.55 — a combination of deposits from her family members, the Australian Taxation Office (ATO), Centrelink payments and wages from different businesses — had been withdrawn from her account. The financial activity strongly supported the police's theory that Hazel and Holdom had stolen Karlie's identity after she was murdered to take money Karlie would have been entitled to if she'd been alive.

Karlie's card had been used in a range of smaller transactions at stores and ATMs in 2008 and 2009. Many of the purchases were linked to Holdom, including TV rental at the Royal Adelaide Hospital when he was a patient undergoing treatment for kidney problems. The card was also used at a tobacconist not far from Holdom and Hazel's Adelaide home in 2010, and to book a seat on a flight from Canberra to Adelaide in 2012 — Holdom was a passenger on that flight. Sometimes Holdom's bank account was accessed right after Karlie's at the same location.

There were dozens of similar examples, suggesting to police that Holdom either had access to both accounts or that Karlie was still alive at that point. Based on the fact that no one other than Holdom had seen Karlie since December 2008, the latter seemed extremely unlikely to police.

Of all the money that had flowed in and out of Karlie's account after her death, the most chilling transaction was a deposit on 15 September 2010. On the same day the deposit was made, $500 was withdrawn from Karlie's account at an ATM at the Elizabeth Park shopping centre in Adelaide's northern suburbs.

'What's of interest in relation to this transaction is that the money has been deposited by Karlie's mother,' Detective Huppatz said, staring at Holdom. 'It suggests to me that Karlie's mother believes Karlie is still alive because she's had a request from [someone] who she thinks is Karlie to have some money placed into her account.'

He paused for effect before cutting to the chase. Essentially someone, Huppatz said, had asked Karlie's mother to put money into the account of her daughter, who at the time was dead. 'Now you've said to us that at this point you're in control of this account.'

The phone call had been made in September 2010 — two weeks after Karlie's bones had been found in the Belanglo State Forest.

Holdom avoided the question and rambled on about his break-up with Hazel in 2011 and how Hazel also had access to Karlie's card.

Detective Huppatz steered the conversation back. 'So it's not you doing that?' he pressed.

'No,' Holdom answered, shaking his head.

'Okay, so possibly Hazel has somehow contacted Karlie's mother and requested she be sent $500, or $500 [be] deposited into Karlie's account,' the detective said.

Holdom didn't know how to respond. He appeared to teeter between denying knowledge altogether or putting the blame on Hazel. 'I don't know what for, we had money back then,' he offered weakly.

The answer revealed nothing but the detective moved on. Holdom had used Karlie's account to deposit his own wages into, from working odd jobs, mainly in construction, up until 2012. There were also large deposits from the ATO, ranging from $5000 to $12,500.

Holdom readily admitted he'd set up a scam that involved registering different businesses, with different directors — like Karlie, Hazel and her sister — and then claiming GST refunds from the ATO. One company called KP Drilling, with Karlie Pearce-Stevenson listed as the director, had been set up after she was murdered. But Holdom claimed Karlie was alive at the time and well aware of the fraud.

There appeared to be a hint of boasting as he told the detectives he managed to squeeze up to $400,000 out of the ATO and had handed out money to his friends. He'd take a small cut, a couple of grand here and there, and his friend, whoever's name he'd registered the company in, would keep the rest.

'It was free money,' Holdom told the detectives. 'Well, it comes out of taxpayers' money, but I guess there's about seven people from Adelaide I did it for, another five, six in Canberra.'

This was how the money turned up in Karlie's bank account, Holdom claimed — she was in on it. Perhaps what he didn't count on was police looking at where that money was then transferred to, including Holdom's own bank account.

In May 2011, there was $22,500 deposited into Karlie's account by the ATO in three separate transactions. Bank records showed $12,500 was then transferred from Karlie's account into a National Australia Bank account registered in Tin Can Bay in Queensland, where Holdom had set up accounts during his time living there in 2004. Holdom claimed he hadn't used that account since then. He admitted he'd skimmed a bit off the top of those ATO payments but that Karlie received the bulk of the money; she used her own bank card to make withdrawals.

Sometimes Holdom went to the bank with her, he said, but he stood outside while she withdrew the money from the teller, especially when it was large amounts they couldn't get out of an ATM in one go.

When the detectives pressed him for more detail, asking him about transaction after transaction, Holdom stuttered and floundered.

'So you don't get the money on her behalf and give it to her?' Detective Gunn asked.

'No. Oh, um, at the end I do,' Holdom replied unconvincingly. 'Like the first one she gives me, like we drew money out, I get my bit, she has her bit.'

Detective Gunn persisted. 'So the money doesn't go to an account that you have?'

Holdom answered, 'No, no.'

Among the hundreds of transactions police had pinpointed, some had been made in Tewantin in Queensland, an hour's drive from Hazel's hometown of Tin Can Bay.

'I think what I'm trying to say here, Daniel, is I suspect that you and Hazel were using Karlie's card,' Detective Huppatz said. 'And further to that I believe that possibly Hazel was passing herself off as Karlie.'

Holdom denied the suggestion, even though he'd chopped and changed his story between keeping Karlie's card, mailing it back to Canberra and giving it back to her in person.

When then, Detective Huppatz asked, was the absolute last time you saw Karlie and Khandalyce?

It was at the Elizabeth Shopping Centre towards the end of 2009, Holdom said, when they'd withdrawn a large amount of money in two separate transactions hours apart. He'd snuck off from the home he shared with Hazel in Hillbank to see Karlie and her daughter one last time.

He recalled Khandalyce was dressed in a Dora the Explorer T-shirt. Perhaps he was unaware that the same type of T-shirt was found in the suitcase with Khandalyce's bones. Holdom claimed that he and Karlie split the cash; she was happy and planned to go to Queensland with a couple of boys she'd met. She left her bank card with him because she was going to get a new one anyway.

'Yeah, the same as I did with everyone, I kept everyone's cards. Youse have arrested me with that many cards it's not funny,' Holdom explained. He kept the bank cards of the people he committed tax rip-offs for so he could use their identity, he said.

***

The detectives also now knew that, in 2013, Holdom had been pulled over randomly by police on the New South Wales Central Coast. During a search of his car, Karlie's bank card was found along with an ice pipe, drugs, and a fuel card from his former employer, Monarch Building Solutions. At the time, Holdom told the officers the bank card belonged to his ex-girlfriend.

The police couldn't have known that the ex-girlfriend Holdom referred to — Karlie — was actually dead and that her remains had been uncovered in the Belanglo State Forest three years earlier. But if Karlie had remained a missing person after her mother's report to Northern Territory

Police in 2009, a search of her name on the police database would have raised a red flag.

Instead, the card was destroyed and Holdom was charged with a string of petty offences, none of which had anything to do with Karlie's disappearance.

* * *

Periodically throughout the afternoon, when the recording discs needed to be changed or Holdom looked like he needed a break, detectives Gunn and Huppatz left the interview room to call and update their respective teams in Sydney and Adelaide.

Back at the State Crime Command, Gunn's bosses were anxiously waiting to see what Holdom would say and whether he'd turn out to be the man they'd suspected. The fact that he'd agreed to be interviewed in the first place, without a lawyer, was intriguing.

As well as relaying information back, Gunn and Huppatz used the breaks to find out what evidence other investigators had uncovered throughout the day.

During one of these breaks, the detectives learned that Hazel had told police about finding, in 2010, dozens of disturbing photographs, including the images of Karlie that Hazel had described.

Armed with that information but stopping short of revealing it all, Detective Huppatz said to Holdom: 'This is probably a bit distasteful but I'll go onto a subject here,' he began. 'During your relationship with Karlie, did you ever take nude photographs of her?'

Yes, Holdom admitted he had, but mostly videos in the bedroom, never out in the open or in 'bush scenes'.

The detective asked if he'd ever had any 'unlawful interaction' with Khandalyce?

No, Holdom repeated four times.

'I fucked up once going down this path,' he said, referring to his recent conviction for child sexual assault.

Staying on Khandalyce's case, Detective Huppatz explored whether Holdom could be tied to any of the clothing found with her bones in the suitcase. There were dresses, T-shirts and a blanket — items one could assume a mother would buy her daughter, but there was also a pair of satin Holden-branded boxer shorts. South Australia was Holden's home state; the company employed thousands of workers and had a wide following; Detective Huppatz wanted to gauge whether Holdom was a fan.

'Yeah, Holden through and through, I hate Fords and despise them,' Holdom stated proudly. Karlie was a Holden fan too, he said, and he took the kids shopping and decked them out in Holden gear.

'So you reckon you bought Holden shorts for Khandals?' Detective Huppatz queried.

Yes, Holdom confirmed, he'd bought the shorts for Khandals, Lauryn and his cousin Christine's kids.

It was nearing 6:30 pm and the interview had been underway for several hours. Taking a break for forty-five minutes, Detective Gunn checked in with Detective Dickinson on the phone. As the raids in South Australia and Canberra wrapped up for the day, more information was streaming in about what Holdom had confessed to regarding Karlie's and Khandalyce's deaths over the years. Hazel's evidence had been telling as was the handwritten entry in Toni Blundell's diary.

Armed with the new information from Hazel's interview and the search warrants in the ACT, the detectives walked back into the interview room. Hazel had claimed that Holdom knew Belanglo State Forest well, having spent time there as a kid, and that he'd formed an unnatural infatuation with the case of serial killer Ivan Milat.

It was Detective Gunn's turn to question Holdom.

'Have you ever been to the Belanglo State Forest in New South Wales?' he asked.

'No, I don't know where it is,' Holdom replied. 'Where is it in New South Wales?'

Detective Gunn humoured him, telling Holdom it was in the Southern Highlands between Campbelltown and Goulburn. 'The Belanglo Forest is quite famous for the backpacker murders involving Ivan Milat, which you may or may not have heard of, I don't know,' he said.

Holdom had a recollection. 'I've heard of him eight years ago, I think.'

'Did you have anything to do with Karlie's death?' Detective Gunn asked in an unexpected change of direction. In case police never got the chance to speak with Holdom again, it was incumbent on them to cut to the chase before the interview ended.

Holdom was taken aback. 'No, I did not have nothing to do with her death,' he said. 'I've never harmed a person like that, never physically, no.'

Gunn persisted. 'Are you aware of any other person having been involved or having something to do with her death?'

'No, I never knew anyone wanted her death.'

Holdom denied he'd had anything to do with dumping Karlie's body in the forest either. Detective Huppatz followed up with the same line of questioning about Khandalyce and drew the same denials. He suspected Khandalyce was killed after leaving her mother and a 'natural inference', Detective Huppatz said, was that Holdom was involved in disposing of Karlie's body in the forest and murdering her daughter en route to South Australia.

'I didn't have nothing to do with it, they were both alive every time I've seen them,' Holdom said.

'Did you kill her?'

'No.'

'Did you place her body in a suitcase?'

'No.'

'And dump it on the side of the road?'

'No.'

Holdom stuck by his rebuttals but offered up an unlikely alibi. A man with a grey beard who worked behind the counter at a sex shop in Elizabeth, with a Thai massage parlour out the back, could attest to sighting Karlie and Khandalyce in 2009. They'd both sat and waited in the car outside while he went and bought Viagra. He couldn't remember the man's name but he was 'a dirty old man', 'fifty, sixty, maybe', 'Australian', and came up to Holdom's chin in height.

The alibi sounded far-fetched.

The interview was reaching its final stages and the detectives laid their cards on the table. They told Holdom there'd been detectives in the Northern Territory interviewing people he knew, a search warrant carried out at Hazel's house, and other searches at his old friend Mark Ashman's home, his cousin Christine and Dereck's house, and Toni Blundell's home up the road. Many of those people had provided statements to police.

Holdom's eyes widened and he rubbed his left hand firmly across his forehead.

'So in the fullness of time we'll have a complete picture of what's been going on in relation to this investigation,' Detective Huppatz said.

They also had been told about an SD card, Detective Gunn explained, that apparently had images of Karlie, naked from the waist down with a bottle positioned between her legs. She was dressed in a T-shirt, and when the photo was taken, appeared to be either dead or unconscious.

'I never took that photo,' Holdom offered quickly.

Detective Gunn went on. 'There's also a second image that's been described to the police today as a young female, that looks like Karlie, lying on one side with her leg straight out and one leg bent next to the fallen log, and there's hair covering her face.'

Holdom shook his head. He'd never show a picture like that to anyone, he claimed.

While the interview had been going on, police in New South Wales had also searched Alex's house. Inside a bag of Holdom's possessions was Khandalyce's birth certificate.

'I can't think of why it'd be there,' said Holdom, appearing clueless.

Holdom had kept two suitcases full of his possessions — glass ornaments, car racing star Peter Brock pictures, Roosters rugby league team memorabilia — at his cousin's house in Charnwood in 2008. In 2012, he'd found the bags, moved them to Toni's house and then packed them in a Mazda hatchback when he drove up to the New South Wales Central Coast. Khandalyce's birth certificate must have been mixed up among his belongings in Charnwood, he said, from when she stayed there with her mother, and accidentally moved to the caravan park with him, he reasoned.

Detective Gunn put it to Holdom that he'd spoken to people about killing Karlie and Khandalyce in December 2008, and yet now he was trying to make it appear they were still alive.

'I promise you I did not. Like I said, I swear on my daughter like I did not have anything to do with killing anyone, I couldn't bring myself to kill anyone,' he pleaded.

The detectives warned they'd review the interview and potentially return for a second interview. Until then, Holdom would remain a suspect in the murders.

They began closing their notebooks and pushing out their chairs to stand up.

'But once I've cleared, like once I've shown that she was in Adelaide with me, like, does that still remain?' Holdom asked.

If he could prove Karlie did board a bus to Adelaide from Canberra after December 2008 then yes, that would work in Holdom's favour, Detective Huppatz said.

The interview ended at 8:22 pm.

Chapter 25

Investigators from Strike Force Malaya huddled around a desk telephone in a Homicide Squad meeting room. Teleconferences were being held twice daily between investigators in New South Wales, South Australia and the ACT in order to process the volume of critical information streaming in.

Detectives Willing and Dickinson were present, along with Detective Gunn, bleary eyed after only a few hours' sleep following his seven-hour interview with Holdom. An intelligence analyst was seated at one end of the table, studiously taking notes as the results of the previous day's raids were discussed. It had been twenty-four hours since police had revealed the breakthrough in the cases of Karlie and Khandalyce and twenty-four hours since key suspects in the case had their secrets exposed. The information that had come in from officers on the ground at the searches, and from witnesses, was overwhelming. It was clear there were several people who'd had suspicions about what had happened to the mother and daughter but had failed to come forward either out of fear, self-interest or both.

Detective Bray was hooked up to the teleconference from Adelaide and Detective Sergeant Donna Parsons had tuned in from Canberra. Midway through the discussion, Detective Bray paused as someone interrupted with an urgent update. Hazel Passmore's sister, Amanda Evans, had just walked into a police station in South Australia and handed over an SD card — the same card Hazel had told investigators about.

The existence of that SD card, with photographs of Karlie's body, had been one of the key revelations uncovered during the raids. Investigators had known that finding it would be crucial but they also knew it was a long shot — Holdom had a habit of keeping dozens of SD cards and spread his possessions across different properties and cities. Odds were, the card had been lost years ago and police would only have Hazel's word for what she'd seen on it.

But Hazel had lied to police when she claimed she didn't know where it had ended up. In truth, petrified of what Holdom was capable of, she'd handed it over to her sister in 2012, telling her to keep it in case anything happened to her.

The fact that the card had now been voluntarily handed in to police and still contained some of the chilling and confronting photographs of Karlie was a miracle.

Detective Bray broke the news to the other investigators before making sure that Amanda didn't walk out of the regional police station without making a formal statement. She told police she'd been worried about Hazel, but judging by Hazel's evidence, the relationship between the sisters was unsteady. They'd grown up together in Queensland and settled separately in South Australia as adults. Amanda had been one of Hazel's main supporters when she'd been released from hospital in 2008 and after Holdom took off to the ACT. But something had soured between the siblings, and when Hazel spoke about Amanda, there was malice and mistrust in her voice. She held a grudge against her sister for not telling her about Holdom getting together with Karlie. 'I don't think she cares about much other than herself really,' Hazel said of her sister.

When the State Electronic Evidence Branch in Sydney examined the card, officers were able to recover both the existing and deleted images. The depravity worsened with each photo. The images had been captured on a digital camera at 11:23 am and 11:24 am on 15 December 2008. A close-up photograph of Karlie's upper body and face, with a leg and foot placed over her neck, was captured at 11:31 am on the same day.

The last photograph in the sequence depicted Karlie on her back lying next to a large log; there was foliage on the ground, it was broad daylight and she was naked from the waist down. Her face wasn't visible, but she was wearing a white and pink T-shirt with the word 'Angelic' in cursive writing across the chest — the same T-shirt police had found five years earlier, not far from a female's skeleton in a lonely pocket of the Belanglo State Forest.

Police compared the photographs with the crime scene images taken at the Red Arm Creek Firetrail when Karlie's bones were found in August 2010. The positioning of her body was almost identical.

'Seeing the remains of Angel lying next to a log with those photos, and all these years later you see Karlie's body with the T-shirt in exactly the same location,' Detective Willing later recalled. 'It was a really surreal moment.'

Police were able to recover a series of other deleted photographs on the SD card that formed further links to Holdom: images of Hazel and her daughter, Lauryn; of Holdom at properties he lived at in South Australia and the ACT; and of a skull fragment found on the roadside in Indulkana after the 2008 fatal car crash.

***

It had been twenty-four hours since police had turned up on the doorstep looking for the documents that Alex had collected from the Blue Bay Caravan Park for Daniel Holdom years earlier. At the officers' request, Alex fetched the papers, among them Khandalyce's birth certificate, and handed them over.

Alex — whose identity has been suppressed by a court order — had no idea Karlie and Khandalyce had even been missing. Holdom hadn't mentioned their names since late 2008, when he'd introduced Alex to the young mother and her daughter.

Now seated across from Detective Senior Constable Anthony Moore during an interview, Alex spoke about that brief encounter.

Alex saw Holdom every now and then. Sometimes they'd go for two years without talking until, out of the blue, Holdom would call. In late 2008, Alex recalled, Holdom had called in a panic. 'I've had a car accident and two of the children have died,' he said.

In November 2008, Alex travelled down to Adelaide for the children's funeral, which had been postponed until Hazel was well enough to leave hospital.

'When I arrived, there was a girl named Karlie in the motel room. Karlie had a young daughter with her.'

Holdom claimed that Karlie was there to escape a volatile boyfriend.

'While I was there Karlie received two phone calls on her mobile phone,' Alex said. 'She was hanging up on the calls and threw her phone.'

'Is that him again?' Holdom asked, and Karlie said yes.

'The room was dirty and there were bags of clothes around like it was all of her belongings. I saw that Karlie was colouring a sign that was going to be used for the funeral of Ryan and Willow.'

Karlie's daughter was a 'happy little thing' but Alex was critical of Karlie's parenting, claiming that Karlie put Khandalyce in the shower and left her there, sitting on the floor.

When Alex asked Karlie if she was going to get her out, the young mother replied: 'She can fucking stay in there.'

It was contrary to other accounts police would receive about Karlie, who was more often described as a doting and caring mother. Alex would also be one of only two witnesses who brought Karlie's parenting into question. The other witness was Holdom.

Alex also told the detective about going to Ryan and Willows' funeral in Adelaide, and watching Holdom 'hanging his head' because he felt everyone judging him.

After Holdom left Adelaide with Karlie, Alex had to tell Hazel he'd gone. '[He] never mentioned Karlie or her daughter to me again.'

That was until Holdom called from Cessnock jail to say he was about to be charged with two counts of murder.

Chapter 26

The note in his trembling hands was damp with sweat. A bright, clinical light hanging above the table cast dark shadows over Holdom's face as he fiddled with the paper.

Flustered and tugging at his sweatshirt, he asked Detective Gunn and Detective Sergeant Tim Attwood if they could turn the air-conditioning on. However, the sound of the clunky old unit would overpower the audio recorder capturing the interview, they said; Holdom would have to remain uncomfortable.

For the second time in a week, Holdom was sitting before two homicide investigators inside Cessnock Police Station. He stammered as he tried to explain why he'd asked Detective Gunn to return and hear him out again.

'To give you more, um, background on what I told youse last time we were here in relation to Karlie and Khandals, the murders youse are investigating.' Holdom's eyes darted around the room. 'Um, my main concern is that my name doesn't get brought up in the press 'cause where I am and that. I'll give youse, youse will have a definite lead after what I've told you.'

After the first interview, Detective Gunn had left his card with Holdom and asked him to call if anything else came to mind. Holdom had been escorted back to Cessnock jail but moved into isolation, away from the general prison population for his own protection.

The mystery surrounding the deaths of Karlie and Khandalyce continued to dominate the front pages of newspapers around the country. The community response had been overwhelming, and there was a national outpouring of grief for the heinous manner in which the mother and child had been killed and discarded. People who had never met the girls mourned their loss. Strangers dedicated songs to Karlie and Khandalyce, sketched their faces in sombre artworks, wrote poems, set up tribute pages online, and reached out to family and friends to offer help in any way they could.

While Holdom's name had been kept out of the press, police suggested they were pursuing one very strong line of inquiry. It didn't take long for inmates at Cessnock to put two and two together. Holdom's cell had been raided, and he was absent for several hours after being taken away by police on the same day the identities of the young mother and toddler were revealed.

Now, as well as being a child molester, Holdom had been tagged a child killer — a title that left him vulnerable to inmates dishing out their own interpretations of justice. You could kill another man, smuggle kilograms of drugs into the country or hold up a service station, and sail through your jail term, but the buck stopped at violence against children. Even the hardest of criminals had standards.

While Holdom had been tucked away in solitary confinement for seven days, he'd had plenty of time to think about his first interview and repeated denials. No doubt he could only imagine what evidence police were gathering while he was locked up with no way of saving himself. He needed a plan.

On the night of 27 October, he had sat down on the edge of his mattress inside his cold, concrete cell, and with notepad and pencil he began to write. The following morning, Holdom called a prison officer and handed over the contact details for Detective Gunn.

'I told him, I was insistent like I know it's not a good look, like a dog in a criminal world,' Holdom explained to Detectives Gunn and Attwood. 'And going against me family was even a more heartbreaking thing for me to do, but I just …'

After receiving the call from Corrective Services, Detectives Gunn and Attwood jumped in an unmarked police car and sped up the M1 towards the Hunter region. Given Detective Attwood's history with the Angel case, he'd been brought on to Strike Force Malaya to work alongside Detective Gunn. They'd been dissecting Holdom's first interview, a time-consuming process that involved discounting or proving his claims.

But the detectives were in a different position this time around. They'd since received phone data records from Holdom's and Karlie's mobile phones from 2008, and as they made their way up to Cessnock the information was being analysed. There were also witness statements claiming Holdom had left Canberra with Karlie and returned without her. Coupled with Holdom's damning first interview in which he'd provided wildly conflicting versions, a circumstantial case for Karlie's murder was emerging.

Khandalyce's case, on the other hand, would need a bit more work. While police knew where her body was found, they didn't believe she was killed in Wynarka. Retracing the path of Holdom's phone activity would be key to solving that mystery.

At 1:46 pm on Wednesday, 28 October, Detective Gunn started the second police interview with Holdom.

'Mr Holdom, earlier today I received contact from the Department of Corrective Services who indicated to me that you wished to speak with police further. Is that the case?' Detective Gunn asked.

'Yes.' Holdom nodded.

'And what is it that you wish to tell us today?'

Holdom looked down at the seven pages containing lines of his barely decipherable handwriting. 'Youse are already aware, like, you already touched on things last time we spoke and you knew I didn't know the answers to it,' he said.

With a deep inhale, Holdom began to unload on Dereck Dover, the man who had put a roof over his head whenever he needed it and defended him when no one else would. The last time Holdom had seen Karlie and Khandalyce, he claimed, was before Dereck drove them to a bus station on the night of 14 December 2008.

'I never saw either of them again,' Holdom blurted. 'He disposed of the car solely by himself. I wasn't there. That's how come I didn't know the aspects of the sale of the car.

'As youse already know, I committed fraud with the card, you know that already, um, and youse will have to verify this. I can't remember what it was, it was either Christmas 2009 or '10 when we bought a VZ Commodore. I went back to the ACT with Hazel and I took Karlie's card back with me and phone. I said, "Look, I don't want no further part in this." I said, "I don't know what you've done, don't care, just whatever."'

Holdom claimed he then went to visit Hazel's grandmother in Hervey Bay in Queensland, but that Dereck insisted on posting Karlie's bank card to him right before Christmas in 2009 or 2010.

'He wanted me to have it to make it look like she's been up there,' Holdom said.

It was also Dereck who got in contact with him, via messages to Hazel's Facebook page, after news broke about a body found in Belanglo State Forest.

'He said, "If anyone knows, if anyone asks you any questions, you don't know nothing about what's been found,"' Holdom said as the detectives calmly took notes.

He laid the blame on Dereck again for how he responded to Northern Territory Police when they called about Karlie's missing person's report in 2009.

'Um, when a missing persons report was made and police contacted Dereck, he frantically messaged me and Hazel again by phone and Facebook, again wanting to talk to me and telling me what to say to them, and give them a number he gave me to give to missing persons.

'I did as I was told. Christine was the one I think who made the family call, 'cause she spoke to missing persons and also sounded like Karlie did.'

Yes, Holdom conceded, he did take money out of Karlie's bank account in Charnwood but it was under duress from his cousin and her husband.

'I'll go Crown witness against them if I have to,' he said. 'I just want me name left out of the thing and try and like,

I'm already into my parole at jail. I want to go into witness protection and yeah, I don't want anyone to find me, not even me own family.'

Holdom stopped talking. There was a longer than comfortable silence in the room as the detectives processed what they had just been told. It sounded like Holdom was hinting at a negotiation.

'You said that you want to talk to us because you are concerned about your name getting out there, and concerned about your name being exposed by something,' Detective Gunn observed. 'Can you just explain to me what you mean by that?'

The detectives were pretty certain Holdom was lying again. He was jumping between topics erratically, stopping midway through one sentence and starting another, and he couldn't maintain eye contact. But he obviously wanted something in exchange for what he was selling as a case-breaking tip-off and a chance to clear his conscience.

'I started watching all the headlines … I thought, so the right thing to do is make the community safe, even though it is turning against my family to say what I know,' Holdom began. 'But when this leads to his arrest once youse get all the facts I just don't want me name brought up 'cause I'm well-known all through the jail system and I'll fear for my safety even more.

'Once I've helped youse, done the right thing by Corrective Services, they're going to try to vouch for me to get my manifest injustice signed and for my CORE group at Surry Hills or somewhere else.'

Holdom had been eligible for parole in September 2015, but his release had been knocked back because he hadn't yet completed a sex offender's treatment program (CORE). In

New South Wales, an offender denied parole has to wait twelve months before they can be considered for release again, unless they can prove a 'manifest injustice'. That meant proving the parole board either refused Holdom's release on false, misleading or irrelevant information or its concerns could be addressed in a way that warranted reconsideration.

Holdom thought he could use the investigation as his ticket out of there; if he helped police they could ask the parole board to reconsider his release from jail. Once he was out, he also expected New South Wales Police to pay for his new life in witness protection.

'So is it the case that you have written this information and are telling us this because you want to protect your prison classification, or are you telling us because it's the truth?' Detective Gunn asked.

'It is the truth,' Holdom quickly offered.

'Right,' Gunn responded cautiously.

'It's the truth. Youse already knew from the start when I was lying, you know I wasn't there for certain things.'

Holdom handed Detective Gunn the seven pages of his handwriting, riddled with spelling mistakes and abbreviations. The uncorrected confession read:

Two parts you can already confirm and know. I was no there for the sale of the car as youse already know.

I knew little facts of the transaction and my story did not match his missing persons statement.

I split from Hazel. I went to the ACT. I got cash from acc [account] so they could have money. After that I refused to do it anymore.

I wanted no part of it from there. We had fallout and weren't getting along.

There will be traces of money transfers sent to Charnwood Post Office for Christine and Dereck and there is money put into Dereck's ANZ accounts their others too for them.

That is on top of cash fro them.

The phone was treated like debit card. Christine was the one who made calls to family and spoke to Missing Person as she sounded like Karlie.

I eventually formed a relationship with Toni and moved out of my cousin's place.

It caused even more conflict. I ended up leaving ACT to Central Coast and ended up in gaol. Around eight months or so I sent a letter to Hazel if she help me financially and I never heard back and phone calls have been rejected since.

Approx four months ago I sent a letter to Dereck to see if he could financially help me after all I have done for him.

I got no reply. A couple of months after that is when the case was on the news.

Your first link which youse already know, I never saw K or K again after Dereck said he took them to the bus stop. He disposed her car directly after for no reason and onto an older car.

Youse already know I was not there for the sale of the car due to my lack of knowledge of transaction details.

So yea, I did lie when I said I there for it. I kept her card and eventually committed fraud with it as I was committing tax fraud for several people at the time. Christmas 2009 or 2010 when the VZ was bought from Jarvis Ford I went back to ACT on way to Queensland for holidays to Hazel's grandparents' house at Hervey Bay.

When in ACT I told Dereck I wanted no further part in this and handed card back to him and I left.

He kept calling and messaging telling me I was already part of it. He wanted an address so he could send the card to so I could use it there in Queensland.

I gave him Hazel's grandparents' address.

It arrived approximately the same or next day it arrived. He sent package from Charnwood.

I think it was reg [registered post] I ain't sure, I don't remember if I used card or not. When remains were found in the forest, Dereck sent frantic messages on Hazel's Facebook on phone to contact me. He said is anyone said anything about it to say nothing. You should be able to trace messages or msg and contact.

When missing persons report was made and contacted Dereck, he frantically messages me and Hazel by phone on Facebook wanting to talk to me and telling me what to say to them and give them a number he gave to me to give to Missing Persons.

I did as I was told. I believe that number was my cousin who spoke to them.

I want my manifest injustice signed and out of gaol. I want witness protection. I don't to be in this state at all, I want my name change.

I don't want my name in media and I will fill all the missing links for youse.

Holdom sounded pleased with himself. 'Yep, that's what I've done there,' he said. Gunn finished reading the letter for the record and asked Holdom to sign, date and number the pages with blue ink pen.

He then began to pick apart the lies in forensic detail.

'Do you recall telling me in the first interview that you had seen Karlie attend [sic] Adelaide with Khandalyce on a bus, and that was in early 2009?' Detective Gunn asked. 'Is that true?'

'No,' Holdom replied.

'Do you recall telling me in that first interview that Karlie and Khandalyce were living and staying in the Adelaide area from early 2009 towards the last quarter of 2009 around October? Is that true?'

'No, ah, it's not true.'

The detective began to recite the dishonest answers Holdom had provided during the first interview: Holdom paid $560 for Karlie to stay in a motel in Canberra in 2008; that he spent time with Karlie in Adelaide in 2009 and had her permission to trade in her car.

Yes, Holdom confirmed, all lies. But he had told the truth about how he got together with Karlie, the use of her bank cards from 2008 onwards, how he crashed a car and killed Hazel's two children and that he was a drug dealer at the time.

After the body was found in the Belanglo State Forest in 2010 and the story hit the news, Holdom said he was bombarded with messages from Dereck telling him to keep his mouth shut.

'I had a feeling something was wrong, but the less I knew, the better I thought I was,' he said.

Dereck had taken Karlie to the bus stop after their argument over rent, made sure she had a ticket, and they agreed he could sell her car to cover the money she owed him. Holdom was just following orders, and while he thought something was not quite right when Dereck pulled out her mobile phone and bank card twenty-four hours later, he kept quiet.

'I thought he was just going to kick her out, I didn't know he'd put her on a bus,' he said. After all, his interest in Karlie had been sexual. 'I was just rebounding more than anything.'

Detective Attwood asked Holdom what his emotional feelings were for Karlie.

'Oh, it wouldn't have really mattered if I did have her or didn't have her,' he answered offhandedly. 'I guess I was looking for someone to lean on.' In his mind, it was never going to last.

At this point, Holdom, in his new story, hadn't addressed what had happened to Khandalyce; the toddler had been completely left out of his letter.

There was a sense of scepticism in Attwood's voice as he asked Holdom why Karlie would get on a bus without her young daughter. 'Did you think it was unusual?' he asked.

'To leave her daughter behind?' Holdom replied.

Attwood repeated his query. 'Yes, leave Khandalyce.'

Holdom seemed caught off guard by the line of questioning. 'She took Khand ... both, yes they both went,' he finally blurted.

'If that was the case, did you assume Dereck was going to bring them back?'

'I didn't know exactly where he was taking her,' Holdom replied. 'I didn't want to take sides. Um, I did think it was strange when he came back without her but he said she's on a bus, she's gone somewhere.'

Holdom never confronted Dereck about Karlie and Khandalyce's whereabouts because he didn't want to start a fight, he said. He'd already had a scuffle with Dereck's brother in the past and he wasn't prepared to go round two.

'I know Dereck's got something to do with it now, it's all coming together,' Holdom said. 'It's the best thing in the community's interest that I do the right thing and tell youse what, as much as I know and what I did and what my part was. I thought if it was my kid I'd want someone to tell me what went on …'

A beeping from the audio recorder brought the interview to a halt — the discs would run out of recording space in five minutes and needed to be changed over. The interview was put on hold. Holdom gulped down a glass of water while detectives Gunn and Attwood left the room to discuss what they'd just heard.

In fact, midway through the interview, Gunn had received a message. The phone records had been analysed and there was new and compelling evidence.

Now Gunn spoke to Detective Dickinson, who was back at the offices in Parramatta. Dickinson told him that Holdom's phone records showed he was in the vicinity of Belanglo State Forest around the time Karlie was killed.

Karlie's phone activity had showed a similar pattern; it registered with cell towers from Canberra's northern suburbs in the early hours of 15 December 2008 through to the Southern Highlands, and finally in the vicinity of the Belanglo State Forest.

It was powerful evidence that all but proved Holdom was with Karlie when she had last been seen alive and in the place her body was found. The detectives discussed the evidence they had so far and what Holdom had spoken about in the second interview. It sounded like more lies. Holdom was no longer just a suspect.

The detectives had reached a point where they had enough evidence to charge him with Karlie's murder, and with the go-ahead from their superiors back in Sydney, detectives Gunn and Attwood walked back into the interview room.

Holdom raised his head and watched the investigators sit down at the table. He appeared to acknowledge the shift in the room.

Detective Gunn held his notebook in his hands. 'Daniel, during the break there have been some developments,' he said slowly and clearly. 'As a result, I have to inform you that you are under arrest for the murder of Karlie Pearce-Stevenson. Do you understand that?'

There was a long pause. 'Yes,' Holdom said finally, stunned.

Detective Gunn cautioned Holdom — if he proceeded to answer questions he would be interviewed as someone under arrest, not just a suspect. A custody officer came into the room and rattled off the standard spiel to Holdom about his rights under arrest, and Holdom indicated he didn't want to continue the interview any further; he wanted legal advice.

'I've already said everything that I believe is true, like I've told youse, um, I've got nothing else to say,' Holdom said without a hint of emotion in his voice. 'I've done nothing wrong, I don't know why youse are accusing me of this.'

Detective Gunn wrapped up the interview and stood, closing his notebook with Holdom's handwritten letter — lightly stained from the oil of his skin and sweat of his palms — vanishing between the pages.

Holdom squirmed uncomfortably in his chair.

As Detective Gunn left the room, Holdom made a last-ditch attempt to proclaim his innocence. 'You've got the wrong guy, you'll see!' he declared.

Chapter 27

Crammed onto the long, uncomfortable benches in Maitland Court House, journalists craned their necks to get a glimpse of him. A handful of cameras had been set up in the neat, garden-lined courtyard outside, reporters filled the public gallery and detectives loitered in the hallway outside, weary from the long week.

Most days the country courthouse dealt with petty crimes. A dozen or so locals would pass through the towering terracotta archway and file into the timber-panelled courtroom to answer to allegations of drink-driving, speeding or shoplifting. As the closest courthouse to Cessnock Police Station, it was also the first place offenders appeared after being arrested and charged if they were refused bail.

For days leading up to 28 October 2015, there had been speculation in the media about an imminent arrest. On 22 October, the *Sydney Morning Herald* published a story revealing the investigation had progressed at a rapid pace and police had identified a suspect, who was in custody for unrelated offences. The next day, the story was updated: the suspect was serving time behind bars in New South Wales for child sex offences.

Publicly, detectives said they were keeping an open mind but, behind the scenes, Holdom — whose name had remained out of the press — was their number-one suspect.

Then, on 27 October, the day before Holdom had been charged with Karlie's murder, Detective Des Bray held a sensational press conference in Adelaide and detailed the fraud that had been carried out in Karlie's name after her death. He also revealed that her phone had been used to provide proof of life to family and friends after the mother and daughter had been murdered.

The unusually revealing press conference had been a goldmine for reporters, but caused some angst among New South Wales homicide detectives, who thought they might have given away too much too soon.

Now, the morning after Holdom's second police interview, reporters were growing impatient as the accused's legal-aid lawyer explained to the magistrate that his client didn't want to appear in court in person.

Journalists held their breath, hoping the magistrate would not concede to the request; they wanted to see the accused man in the flesh so they could describe his appearance and his reaction in the courtroom. A sketch artist hired by one of the commercial TV stations was there to record the accused's likeness — if the man didn't appear the long drive from Sydney would have been a waste of time.

'Given the nature of the charge, I think it's appropriate he be brought on screen,' Magistrate John Chicken said, noting it was a matter of some notoriety. 'It is not like he is being brought in and paraded.'

There was mutual relief at the compromise. Holdom wouldn't make it to court in person but he would appear by audio-visual link from the watch house cells downstairs.

As the TV mounted on the wall flickered, faces were raised. When Holdom, dressed in a green fleece jumper, appeared on the screen, the room was silent for a moment, bar the sound of the sketch artist hastily scratching pencil across paper.

An adjournment was sought until 12 November at Central Local Court in the heart of Sydney, and the matter was over in minutes. The brief court appearance had been mainly a formality, the beginning of what would be a long process through the justice system.

Holdom only uttered three words but the sound of his deep voice startled some in the gallery. 'Yes, Your Honour,' he said in response to a simple statement about the location of the hearing, before his face disappeared from the TV screen and reporters scurried outside to file updates in the warm spring sunshine.

Holdom would stay in the courthouse cells until a prison truck came to collect him and transport him back to the Cessnock Correctional Centre. There he would be placed in segregation to avoid unwanted attention from fellow inmates when his face appeared on the evening news.

While the arrest of Holdom for Karlie's murder was big news, there was much more groundwork for detectives to cover. No one had been charged for Khandalyce's murder but police now knew it was Holdom.

Behind the scenes, police and the Directors of Public Prosecutions (DPP) in New South Wales and South Australia were negotiating which state would lay the charge for Khandalyce's murder. Detectives were still not sure where the toddler was killed; they knew she left the ACT alive and ended up dead in South Australia, which suggested she'd been killed somewhere in between.

If it was decided that a territorial nexus existed between Khandalyce's murder and New South Wales, then detectives could charge him in that state — regardless of knowing the exact location of her death. South Australia Police would then have to let go of the case and hand over the reins, a move some South Australian investigators were reluctant to do.

'There was legal discussion between the two DPPs, and they agreed the nexus was strong enough to New South Wales that it was appropriate he was charged here,' Detective Willing recalled years later. 'Behind the scenes, that upset some of the police in South Australia, and understandably so. [Detective] Des Bray and I had spoken and agreed — it was what it was, and, at the end of the day, if the evidence pointed to the murder occurring here in New South Wales they would give up the case and give it to us, and vice versa.

'But in my mind it was always going to head in my direction.'

Chapter 28

It had been twelve days since Hazel had a four-hour conversation with detectives in the back of an unmarked police car outside her house. She had offered a lot of information, most importantly revealing the existence of photographs of Karlie when she died.

It was a mixture of sheer luck and quick police work that those photographs fell into the strike force's lap. Uncovering crucial evidence at a crime scene could be difficult and time-consuming twenty-four hours after a murder was committed, let alone seven years after.

When Detective Bridge and Detective Edwards left Hazel's house in Davoren Park on 21 October, they'd asked her to contact them if she had any more information. She did, but next time it was through her solicitor, Patrick Liptak.

Mr Liptak was the Adelaide lawyer who'd worked on the personal injury claim against Holdom over the 2008 car crash. He firmly told police that any communications they needed to have with Hazel would have to go through him. In police slang, Hazel had lawyered up.

While her initial interview had been helpful in parts, it was clear Hazel knew more than she was letting on. Within a couple of days of searching her home, the media had caught on to who Hazel was and how she fitted into the case: the accused killer's ex-girlfriend, who had lost two children in a car crash he'd caused.

Reporters had also drawn a link between Hazel's wheelchair and a description of someone who had committed a fraud in Karlie's name after her murder. South Australia Police had carefully but intentionally pointed out in a press conference that a woman in a wheelchair purporting to be Karlie and with Karlie's identity documents had gone into the Australian Central Credit Union in Elizabeth on 24 June 2010.

Hazel's repeated visits to police stations near her homes after the search warrant, and a bizarre, discreet meeting with her lawyer in a park, away from prying eyes, had only fuelled the suspicion that surrounded her.

Now media were camped outside Hazel's house and the pressure was mounting. While Hazel managed to keep tight-lipped when reporters bombarded her with questions as she got into her car each day, the attention became too much for her partner, James Matheson. At one point he stormed outside and threw eggs from his driveway at media crews and screamed at them to fuck off.

Detectives weren't concerned; the pressure and constant attention would work in their favour. It was abundantly clear that Hazel knew about Karlie's death, probably Khandalyce's also, and hadn't told police. It was puzzling why a woman would choose to stay with someone who'd confessed to murder, but Hazel seemed beholden to Holdom and willing to do anything to ensure he didn't leave her again.

Hazel had had boyfriends before, she told police, but in her eyes, no one compared to 'Danny'; he cared for her, bought her things, took her and the kids out to the park, and promised her the world. It seemed that he was proud to call Hazel his girlfriend and happy to show her off. Ever charming, Holdom made her feel loved, which was something she had seldom experienced before.

When he'd left her in Adelaide after the car crash in 2008, Hazel felt isolated and unsupported; she'd felt discarded like rubbish, while hospital bills piled up around her. Yet when he hinted at coming back to her, she let him walk right back into her life, despite warnings from her friends. When Holdom turned up on her doorstep in the early hours of 20 December 2008, normalcy had returned. Hazel even stood by him when he was sentenced in November 2009 to a paltry eighteen-month good behaviour bond for charges arising from the car crash that killed two of Hazel's children. Hazel didn't feel alone anymore, and she'd been willing to do whatever was needed to keep it that way.

During her first interview, she'd attempted to create ambiguity about what she knew, but police suspected it was a self-serving account. She was trying to protect herself — or, worse, Holdom.

South Australia and New South Wales detectives discussed offering Hazel an inducement — if she told police everything she knew, the statement wouldn't be used as evidence against her. The deal would prevent police from using Hazel's admissions to build a case against her. They knew enough about the case to know Hazel wasn't directly involved in the murders. Phone records and witness accounts placed her nowhere near Belanglo State Forest or the ACT when the crimes were committed. At its highest, she may have concealed a criminal offence.

The inducement was a step short of indemnity from prosecution. If police found evidence elsewhere that implicated Hazel in the crime, she could still be charged. Induced statements are commonplace in homicide investigations, particularly when there is valuable evidence to be gained from a reluctant witness.

At 1 pm on 2 November 2015, Hazel, dressed in a black shirt and a long grey and black striped skirt and with her son on her lap, arrived at Elizabeth Police Station with Mr Liptak and Adelaide silk William Boucaut SC. Mr Boucaut was one of the city's leading criminal barristers and knew how to strike a deal. When he'd worked at the South Australia DPP before moving to private practice, he'd led special projects designed to clear backlogs in the court system by negotiating plea deals with defence lawyers.

Mr Boucaut sat with Hazel inside a tiny interview room towards the rear of the station, away from the prying eyes of the reporters outside the glass sliding doors.

'My understanding is that you have attended here today with your lawyers and wish to provide a statement of your knowledge of Karlie and Khandalyce, and offences committed on Karlie's bank account and Centrelink payments,' Detective Bridge said.

Hazel nodded.

Detective Bridge, who was seated across from Detective Paul Ward, handed Hazel a piece of paper with the conditions of the deal she had agreed to. 'Could you, for the purpose of the tape, read that out for me, and once you have finished, the South Australian one as well,' she asked. It was the start of a lengthy interview that was later tendered in court.

Clearing her throat, Hazel began. 'I am making this statement after a promise held out to me by the New South Wales Director of Public Prosecutions that no information given in it will be used in any criminal proceedings against me in any court in New South Wales, except in the respect of the falsity of my statement or for the purpose of establishing the falsity of evidence given to me as a witness,' she said.

Hazel then read out the South Australian equivalent. In essence, the deal meant Hazel would be protected from being charged with any offence except perjury — she couldn't lie during the interview.

'I just have to reiterate to you that these offences are of the most serious nature, and because of this, it is of the utmost importance that you are truthful in your answers,' Detective Bridge said. 'As you have stated in the reading out of the indemnities, you must remember if you provide a response that is false you may have criminal proceedings brought against you. Do you understand that?'

'Yes,' Hazel confirmed as she anxiously picked her fingernails. 'Don't even know where to start.'

Attempting to put her at ease, Detective Bridge suggested she start with the car accident in September 2008.

Hazel went through the timeline from her stay in the Royal Adelaide Hospital, to Holdom leaving with Karlie for the ACT, to when he returned. It was all background information police had heard before.

Hazel knew why she was there and what the detectives really wanted to hear. She started to explain when Holdom first hinted in 2009 that something had happened to Karlie.

Holdom and Hazel were living in Adelaide's northern suburbs but he would travel to Canberra frequently. She waited until he'd left the house one day and rifled through his car.

'I found one of her cards,' she recalled. 'And I didn't think anything bad at the time. I thought, you know, he was just seeing her and, you know, had lied to me again. He did say then, you know, "No, no, she's gone, she's gone for good." He did admit what he done then, but I didn't believe him. I thought, I don't know if you understand Daniel, but his lies are always extreme.'

Instead, Hazel claimed, she suspected he was secretly dating Karlie.

'He said that, he said that he had raped her with a bottle, he had stomped on her throat and crushed her windpipe,' Hazel said. Tears welled in her eyes and she paused.

'It's all right, Hazel, take your time,' Detective Ward assured her.

Hazel sniffled. 'That was about all he said,' she replied. 'He didn't say too much at all. He just said he'd crushed her throat.'

Detective Ward changed the direction of the interview and took Hazel back to 19 December 2008, when Holdom drove from the ACT to Adelaide via Wagga Wagga. Through Holdom's phone records, police knew he was in constant contact with Hazel during that trip. There were dozens of text messages and phone calls exchanged between the two, but Ward wanted to know what was said in those exchanges and if Hazel knew that Khandalyce was in the car with Holdom at the time.

'I don't remember fighting or arguing or anything like that; yeah, he was being really good and asking about Lauryn,' she said. 'He was bringing presents back for Lauryn.'

Hazel denied knowing Khandalyce was in the back of Holdom's car when she spoke to him as he drove from the ACT towards Adelaide. She did recall hearing children's voices in the background when she spoke to Holdom before he left Dereck's house. Holdom had been sitting in his car in the driveway. Pop singer Rihanna's song 'Rehab' was playing on the car stereo and Hazel assumed the voices she heard were Dereck's kids, not Khandalyce.

When Holdom arrived in Adelaide in the early hours of 20 December 2015, three hours later than expected, he was grumpy. He walked through Hazel's front door, and soon became suspicious that Hazel had been sleeping with a male friend who was also staying at her house. Holdom wasn't up for talking and went to bed immediately.

The detectives wanted as much detail as possible about the twenty-four-hour period leading up to Holdom's arrival in Adelaide — including the many phone calls between them — and vague recollections weren't going to cut it.

'We've got information that Karlie was certainly deceased a couple of days before then,' Detective Ward said. 'And that Khandalyce, you would assume, a two-and-a-half-year-old little girl was missing her mum. She's in a foreign environment and you would suspect, I would have thought, that she would have been pretty upset in the back of the car. Did you hear, at any time, Khandalyce during any of those phone conversations? Because there were quite a few of them.'

Despite being pressed, Hazel was resolute. 'I heard no kids at all or I would have questioned him, or it would have been in the text messages,' she said firmly. 'I would have said something because I would have thought that he was lying to me again and bringing them back together again.'

A car trip from Canberra to Adelaide, along the route Holdom claimed to be taking, should have taken about thirteen hours, but it took him twenty-four hours. If the trip had taken almost twice as long as it should have, and Holdom was providing a constant stream of updates about his progress, surely Hazel would've queried what the hold-up was.

Holdom did suggest he had car problems during the trip, Hazel offered.

Delicately, Detective Ward reminded her about the inducement agreement on the table between them, before he changed tact and asked about Khandalyce. The information Hazel was providing was not adding up.

Referring again to when Holdom arrived in Adelaide, Detective Ward asked: 'Did he say to you anything about Karlie or Khandalyce? Because I think you would have been pretty keen to know what was going on, wouldn't you?'

'Well,' Hazel started, 'as far as I knew she had gone with Daniel to score drugs and she went with the guy and didn't want to come back to Daniel. That was his version of events.'

Hazel and the police knew that version didn't check out as Karlie and Khandalyce were already dead. The challenge was figuring out whether Hazel knew Khandalyce's murder was going to happen before it did.

'Do you know who that guy is?' Detective Ward asked.

Hazel replied, 'No idea.'

'Do you know where that guy is from?'

'No, he didn't mention a name or say anything. That's what made it suss to me, you know.'

'Did you press him on it?'

'Not at that point, at the point I'm on a lot of methadone. I didn't really get it. I didn't really comprehend too much, you know what I mean?'

The interview shifted back to mid-to-late 2009, when Hazel had rifled through Holdom's car and found Karlie's identity documents. The detectives wanted more details on exactly what Holdom admitted to after he said Karlie was 'gone'.

Hazel remembered holding herself up against the Holden Statesman, her sheer grit motivated by an urge to catch Holdom out, and going through the rubbish and bags of clothing while pushing aside work tools in the boot. She found Khandalyce's birth certificate folded up, Karlie's Medicare card and a pension card. It was the same birth certificate police found years later during the search of Alex's house on 21 October 2015.

As a frenzied Hazel rummaged through Holdom's car, brushing aside fast-food wrappers that littered the back seat, she was caught in the act. Unflinching, Hazel unleashed: Why did Holdom have Karlie's things in his car? Was he cheating on her? Was he still seeing her in Canberra?

'And he's like, it's just stuff she's left in the car,' Hazel told the detectives. 'I'm like, "Ah bullshit. She's here, she's here. I know she fucking is," and I was going off my nut and he pulled me inside, literally by the scruff of the neck, and he threw a chair. And once inside he started shaking me, and he's like, "She's disappeared, she's gone, she's dead."

'I didn't comprehend that at all. I'm like, "How did she die?" And that's when he went into fucking … with the bottle and standing on the neck and crushing her throat, or windpipe, I think he put it.'

The gravity of the information was lost in Hazel's deadpan delivery. The question on everyone's mind was why hadn't Hazel come forward?

She claimed she did a bit of Google searching to see if a body had turned up anywhere that would confirm Holdom's story, but that was as proactive as she got.

'To be honest I didn't really want to know if it was the truth, and if it wasn't the truth, well, I didn't need to know he was just lying to me,' Hazel said trying to justify her lacklustre response to the confession.

Detective Bridge, who had been intently listening to the interview and taking notes, stepped in and asked whether Holdom revealed why he did it.

'Um no, well, kind of, but I didn't know whether to believe him, he reckoned he wanted to come back to me,' Hazel said. 'He did it for me, it was all me, and I was like, whatever, "you're a psycho".'

They stayed together, Hazel said, and in 2010 she'd rummaged through his possessions again, but this time in his bedroom. The couple were living in a house on Pacific Boulevard in Hillbank, on the northern outskirts of Adelaide. It had taken a while for Hazel to find the right place. She needed somewhere without stairs, and with hallways wide enough to accommodate her wheelchair. Using money from an insurance payout after the car crash, Hazel paid several months' rent upfront.

But by 2010, Hazel and Holdom were cash poor and struggling to pay the rent on time, even though Holdom was working odd jobs. Hazel knew he had money coming in but suspected he was blowing most of it on drugs, so she went searching for proof.

Yanking out a drawer in a bedside table, she found a small pile of cards. Most were sim cards; unsurprising, given Holdom swapped between mobile phones regularly. But an SD card caught her attention as Holdom wasn't one to take photographs. When Hazel inserted the SD card into a card reader connected to her computer she found it contained dozens of photographs, pornographic images mostly, of young girls and teenagers that Hazel assumed Holdom had downloaded from the internet. Among them were the photos of Karlie, the most disturbing an image of her lying on her back with a glass bottle between her legs.

When Hazel confronted Holdom, initially he denied it was Karlie at all. But Hazel persisted, unwilling to accept his explanation. Finally he confessed: he'd killed both Karlie and Khandalyce, then headed to Adelaide and thrown Khandalyce's body off the highway en route. There was no mention of a suitcase, Hazel claimed.

Given the amount of time that had passed since the conversations occurred, and Hazel's prescription drug use at the time, her memory regarding exact dates was hazy. Some details of Holdom's supposed confession didn't match up with the police theory of what had happened to Karlie and Khandalyce either. Hazel thought Karlie and Khandalyce were both murdered at the same time in the same location, which was at odds with the evidence.

'He was in the forest,' Hazel told the detectives. 'Karlie was still alive; he said she was trying to get to Khandalyce. He said he had to go back and stand on her throat and crush her windpipe to stop her from trying to crawl. She was trying to crawl to Khandalyce while he was hurting her.'

Given Holdom's sexual interest in children, police suspected Holdom tried to abuse Khandalyce before she died. As perverted as the crime was, the detectives needed the minute details of what Holdom had done to the child.

Detective Ward assured Hazel that police were satisfied she was not involved in the murders of Karlie and Khandalyce.

'But there are a lot of things that tell us you probably know quite a bit,' he said. 'Given your intimate relationship with Holdom and his willingness and desire to exchange sexually explicit ideas and material. What I'm asking is, if you do know … I'd like you to be honest and tell me. What did he tell you?'

The words tumbled out of Hazel's mouth before she could stop them. 'He said he sexually abused the body before he dumped her,' she said.

Hazel recalled that Holdom said Khandalyce died 'during it', a reference to the toddler being sexually assaulted.

Detective Ward didn't want to hear a sanitised version from Hazel, no matter how graphic the details were. It was important that Hazel repeated, as much as she could remember, word for word what Holdom told her about Khandalyce's death without sugar-coating it.

'Um, can't even put it into words,' Hazel said. 'He said he was trying to have sex with her, he said something about her crying and stuff. So he made her quiet; he said something about stuffing panties in her mouth. I don't think he said anything about choking, he might have said suffocating. He did say she died, but that was it. Didn't say much after that.'

Holdom's confession had cemented in Hazel's mind that her partner had killed the mother and child, yet she'd still stayed with him.

'It wasn't until the end of 2010 I thought he was capable of it,' Hazel explained. 'I wouldn't have put it past him, but I still didn't actually believe he had done that. I mean, there were no bodies, there was nothing to tell me that he had done that. But yeah, in the back of my mind, technically I knew by the end of 2010 that he was more than capable, and yeah, he probably had, but there was no evidence to support it in my mind.'

Either that or she simply didn't care.

With a nervous laugh, she told detectives she realised she needed to get out of the relationship at that point or she wasn't going to make it. Hazel and Holdom finally broke up in about 2011, but Hazel argued she had been trying to get rid of him for months leading up to that point. He never took no for an answer, turned up at her home to stare through her window, and refused to move his belongings out.

She told the detectives that she left the SD card in a bag of Holdom's possessions, which eventually ended up with her sister, Amanda. It appeared Hazel was trying to play down the suggestion she'd given Amanda the card for safe-keeping because she was in fear of Holdom.

Despite breaking up, and Hazel learning about the murders Holdom had committed, she asked him to look after her daughter, Lauryn, in 2012. It puzzled detectives why any mother would leave their child in the care of someone who had admitted to killing a child.

At the time, Hazel was undergoing an operation in hospital and claimed no one was available to look after her daughter. 'Yes, I had no choice,' Hazel snapped.

'But he's told you he tried to have sex with Khandalyce?' Detective Ward pointed out.

'Yeah, but I didn't, well, I didn't really believe that at the time,' Hazel replied. 'I thought he was off on one of his stories, and you know, making things up. I didn't believe he was capable of doing that.'

It was an answer that contradicted her earlier evidence.

When the news finally broke in 2015 that a suitcase with a child's body inside was found off the Karoonda Highway not far from Tailem Bend, a town Holdom mentioned he had driven through, Hazel began to wonder if it could have been Khandalyce.

Again, Detective Ward asked her why she didn't tell police or anyone about her suspicions. She had been privy to information about two murders but failed to do anything about it.

Attempting to justify her silence, Hazel said she'd found herself on the Crime Stoppers website on several occasions, but couldn't bring herself to make the call. She was scared of Holdom, of the media, of the police, 'of everything'.

Hazel had already spoken openly about her hatred for Karlie. She despised her for leaving with Holdom in 2008 and that resentment never subsided. Racked by jealousy and motivated by revenge, Hazel wanted Karlie to suffer. It raised the question whether Hazel didn't say anything about Karlie's murder because she was simply content with her being out of the picture.

***

'Do you recognise that handwriting at all?' Detective Ward handed Hazel a piece of ripped, lined paper with a few scribbled sentences.

Holdom had left a collection of notebooks scattered across the places he'd stayed at over the years — Dereck and Christine's house in Charnwood; Alex's house; his aunt's house in Canberra. The pages of those books offered a disturbing insight into his sexual desires, the warped and depraved fantasies that inspired his predatory behaviour.

Some of the writings, littered with misspelt words and missing punctuation, read like short stories, and the characters were young women, teenagers and children. In Holdom's fantasies, the children were sexually abused, mistreated for someone else's gratification. Some of the descriptions had striking similarities to what had been done to Karlie in the Belanglo State Forest before she died.

One page, found in his old bedroom at Dereck and Christine's house, included a list divided into four columns. The first column was a list of ages, ranging from two to fifteen years; the second column detailed locations; and the third was full of names. In a fourth column, the words 'rape', 'forced' or 'consent' were scribbled next to the names of the children.

A handwriting expert had compared the writings with other material Holdom had written and concluded it was highly likely Holdom was the author of the lists. The fact his fingerprints were found all over the pages bolstered that view.

The handwriting in most of the notebooks was similar; right leaning, block letters with bold curves, except for the writing in one blue A4 notebook. There, the content echoed the same sentiments — lines and lines of sexual fantasies — but it was clear someone else had penned the stories.

Hazel looked down at the piece of paper, a photocopy of a page from the blue notebook, and paused for half a second. 'Looks like my handwriting,' she said, and lifted her gaze to the detective. 'That's how I do my "s" and stuff. I would say it's mine. It would have been one of his stories that I wrote out for him, I'd say.'

At the behest of Holdom, Hazel had drawn inspiration for these erotic stories from pornography sites and her own personal experiences. Sometimes the stories were typed on a computer and printed out, other times she wrote them in a notebook while Holdom watched.

Detective Ward flicked through six photocopied pages of handwritings uncovered from different notebooks. Some pages had titles, like 'Jones' or 'Mum's Ready' or 'Jay's Mum'. Holdom would ask Hazel to incorporate people from her childhood in the fantasies, such as friends or friends' mothers. Hazel made up the stories, sometimes the names too, in order to go along with Holdom's game and keep him aroused.

While admitting to writing the stories, Hazel claimed she had never seen the list of children's names before. Police had followed up on the names of each child in that list, concerned they may have been the victims of sexual assault. Detectives cross-referenced the towns Holdom had stayed in with the locations on the list, like Taree and Stuart Park, and travelled to each town in a bid to track down the children. But they only had first names to work with. They took it as far as they could but found no evidence that Holdom had abused the children on the list.

* * *

As Hazel's bombshell interview reached its final hours, police turned the line of questioning to the frauds and what role she'd played in impersonating a dead woman.

On 15 December 2010, Hazel and Holdom had walked through the doors of Centrelink in Salisbury. It was the beginning of summer and Adelaide was sweltering; westerly winds whipped up dirt around the streets of the northern suburbs while people huddled under the shade of gum trees.

Hazel had most likely been to Centrelink before to organise government benefits following the birth of her own children, but on that day in 2010, she turned up pretending to be someone else. The welfare agency that day accepted that the person presenting was Karlie Jade Pearce-Stevenson. She was double Karlie's size, brunette not blonde, and wheelchair-bound, but that didn't matter — Hazel didn't need photo identification to carry out what she was about to do.

Under what Hazel suggested was duress, she went into Centrelink purporting to be Karlie to claim an exemption from the child support payment. An exemption entitled Karlie to a back payment for Rent Assistance, and the Family Tax benefit dated back to Khandalyce's birth, four years prior.

By 2010, Karlie had been dead for two years and Holdom had her bank cards. Once Centrelink deposited the back payment into her account, he would simply withdraw it. All he needed was a woman who would pass as Karlie to visit Centrelink and explain the situation.

Holdom knew the welfare system well, having been on a disability support pension for years. He was also a fraudster who had plied a trade of scamming people, but he needed a bit of help sometimes.

When detectives asked Hazel about impersonating Karlie at Centrelink, she claimed she only agreed to do it because Holdom was unrelenting in his requests. He'd told her Karlie had taken off with someone else and that she owed him money so she'd left her card with him. He needed to claw back what was his, he told Hazel. But that was at odds with her earlier evidence that Holdom had told her in 2009 that Karlie was 'gone'.

Hazel claimed she didn't believe him at first, but it was difficult to know whether she was telling the truth. While she knew what she was doing was wrong — impersonating

a single mother to claim her Centrelink benefits —
she despised Karlie. She wanted Karlie to hurt like she did.

'I hated her guts, you know. She destroyed everything I
had and I hated her,' Hazel told police. 'If I could've ripped
money off her I would've done.'

If she was still alive, stealing Karlie's money would cause
her pain, and that alone was Hazel's motivation. She handed
over Khandalyce's birth certificate and Karlie's bank card that
day in Centrelink and doctored a story as to why she needed
the child support exemption. It is unclear what that reason
was but it worked: $7806.70 was paid into Karlie's account.

Hazel admitted she also went to the Australian Central
Credit Union — where Karlie had an account — in Elizabeth
in 2010 with Karlie's bank card and Medicare slip. 'I literally
walked out of the bank and handed him the money straight
outside the bank,' Hazel told police.

While she admitted involvement in the fraud, she
denied playing a role in other impersonations police had
uncovered. On 17 November 2010, Centrelink received a
phone call from someone wanting to change Karlie's address
to where Holdom was living at the time. On 7 December
2010, Centrelink was contacted again and asked to change
Karlie's address to a home where a friend of Holdom's lived.
However, Hazel denied pretending to be Karlie in phone
calls to Karlie's mother and Northern Territory Police. 'No,
no, I never rang anyone,' she said.

Unbeknown to Hazel in the interview room, detectives
had also confirmed she'd started using Karlie's bank card in
early 2009, only a few months after Karlie was murdered.
In January that year, Karlie's account was used to make
purchases from an online gaming website; Karlie had never
used the website, but Hazel did.

Hazel also uploaded Karlie's bank details to her Uber account on 14 January 2009, to pay for travel around Adelaide. It contradicted Hazel's assertion that she'd never spent a cent of the cash from Karlie's account on her own; in her version, it was always handed over to Holdom.

Pressed on this, Hazel told police, sure, Holdom might have bought her a few things but other than that it went to paying rent.

Whether that was true or not, it was hard to tell. Regardless, Hazel had had the satisfaction of causing pain to Karlie, of taking something that was rightfully hers, and that alone was comforting.

Chapter 29

Pink lilies, pale blue hydrangeas and baby's breath adorned the white coffin, a tribute to Karlie's and Khandalyce's favourite colours. A funeral director in Adelaide had organised for it to be custom made. He had never met Karlie or Khandalyce but, like many strangers across the country, was moved by their loss. The coffin was wide enough so Karlie and Khandalyce could be laid to rest together after seven years apart.

It had been a long journey home for the mother and child. Karlie's remains had been at the Glebe Morgue in Sydney and Khandalyce's in Adelaide, where they had been held until final forensic tests were carried out and the bureaucratic processes surrounding repatriation were signed off. The South Australian Victims' Rights Commissioner, Michael O'Connell, and the New South Wales Commissioner for Victims' Rights, Mahashini Krishna, organised that the costs of Karlie and Khandalyce's funeral and repatriation would be covered by victims of crime funds in each state.

The haunting words of Cat Stevens' 'Wild World' rang out inside the Desert Life Church in Alice Springs. It was a song that a young Karlie had sung with her stepfather, Scott. Together they would sit in the backyard, Scott unwinding after work with a beer, and sing together. Little had they known that the song about a young woman venturing out into the world would one day become both a cherished memory and a devastatingly fitting tribute.

Funeral director Meredith Campbell stood before the service with three eulogies before her. The authors of the eulogies, too emotional to read them, had asked Meredith to present the moving tributes on their behalf.

Jade Randle was Karlie's best friend, having gone through Alice Springs High School with her before moving to Adelaide, where she married and had three children. Aside from Holdom, she was one of the last of Karlie's friends to see the young mother alive, and it was her photo of her best friend, taken at Marion shopping centre in Adelaide in November 2008, that police had used in their public appeals. Karlie had just made the long drive to Adelaide from Alice Springs with Khandalyce and looked drained. The photograph showed Karlie with a blank expression on her face, dark circles around her eyes and a mobile phone in her left hand. She wore a black Element-branded singlet and a denim skirt. It was one of the few images the public had seen of Karlie, and did not accurately represent the happy, bright girl her family knew.

Another photograph taken on the same day showed Karlie laughing, a huge toothy grin stretched across her face as she half-turned towards the camera. She looked like a completely different person — playful and carefree. That was the girl Jade would always remember.

'She was little, but her personality and her heart were massive,' Jade wrote in her eulogy. 'She would never let her size stop her from getting what she wanted out of life. She had big dreams.

'We came from a little town called Alice Springs but Karlie knew that there was more and wanted to see the world.

'We always talked about travelling around Australia and someday the world.

'Karlie always knew how to make happiness out of the darkest of situations.' The first time the friends tried smoking cigarettes, Jade said she tried to play it cool but found the head spins nauseating. It was Karlie who tended to her.

'Saying goodbye to someone who meant so much to me is hard, and I never thought I would be the one saying goodbye first.'

To Tanya, Karlie was her best friend's daughter but they also shared a close friendship. In her eulogy she remembered the nights spent out the back of the Poveys' house laughing, talking and singing with whoever wanted to drop by.

Reflecting on Karlie's adventurous spirit, Tanya recounted one memorable camping trip to the Harts Range Racecourse, a two-and-a-half-hour drive from Alice Springs. They hired a small four-wheel-drive and packed one swag between four people. Tanya and Karlie ended up sleeping in the back of the four-wheel-drive, giggling into the early morning, while Scott and Colleen took the swag.

'We didn't sleep much at all,' she wrote. 'We were too busy laughing at all the snoring from the other campers around and listening to the drunk stragglers trying to get back to their camps in the dark after the dance was finished.'

Khandals was a little whirlwind and 'almost ran before she walked'. 'She would look up at Scott like he was a giant, just fascinated with him, and of course she loved her nanna and followed her around everywhere.'

When Colleen died in 2012, Tanya had organised her best friend's funeral, picked out a coffin and carefully selected the flowers. Many of the people who had attended Colleen's funeral were seated around her in the church.

The jolting reminder was equally painful for Scott. Humbly, he always claimed he wasn't much of a public speaker and avoided giving media interviews about Karlie and Khandalyce in case he said something silly that wouldn't do them justice. His self-doubt had kept him quiet but his written word, read out to the service by Meredith, was poignant and deeply touching.

He wrote of finding dead lizards in Karlie's bedroom that she was 'looking after' as a four-year-old child, and the messy room she kept as a teenager that eventually led to him throwing her clothes out the window in protest.

'You took off outside and began to throw them back in as fast as I could get them out, telling me off, and this continued until I started laughing at you. We both cracked up and you promised this time to tidy your room up.'

He treasured the memories of driving road trains with Karlie in the front seat, the desert rushing by. And when Scott, with Luke by his side, and Karlie, aged ten, walked into an open day at St Philip's College, a private school in Alice Springs, Karlie took off at a hundred miles an hour. She ended up on a stage and gave an impromptu performance of the 'Macarena' in front of prospective students and their families, who all laughed affectionately.

'My only regret is that I spent so much time away building the future when I should have been living it preciously instead,' Scott wrote of his long periods away from home working. 'The word love cannot express enough for me. Now in your mum's arms, with Khandals in yours, I wish I could put mine right around you all again.'

Samantha Harris and Karlie grew up as cousins, sharing weekends in the pool and running around Nanna Connie's house, but they were also close friends. When Karlie disappeared, Sam was a driving force in the search for her. She, Tanya and Jade had spearheaded a Facebook campaign, contacting friends and relatives interstate and asking them to be on the lookout for Karlie.

When Khandalyce would have turned six years old, Samantha called schools in South Australia to check if she was enrolled. She hoped she'd catch the mother and daughter out and be able to talk some sense into Karlie about returning home. Above all, she just wanted Karlie to know that she was loved and missed.

Inside the church, Sam, wearing a bright pink dress, placed her hand around a silver handle on the coffin and with five other pallbearers, carried it outside into the waiting hearse. A news photographer across the road captured the twisted anguish on her face and the emotion engulfing everyone else who streamed out of the church that day. The girls had returned home, but in unimaginable circumstances.

Chapter 30

On 15 December 2015 at Parramatta Police Station, on the seventh anniversary of Karlie's murder, detectives charged Daniel Holdom with the murder of Khandalyce. It came after months of discussions between the Offices of the DPP in New South Wales and South Australia over which state should press the charge. It was eventually agreed there was a territorial nexus between the murder and New South Wales. Police believed Khandalyce was killed to cover up her mother's murder and that was sufficient to tie Khandalyce's death to the state.

The decision was made to charge Holdom and continue bolstering the evidence — not an unusual situation in homicide investigations. Police had been poring over Holdom's history looking for tendency evidence — similarities between his prior crimes and the murders of Karlie and Khandalyce. He had a history of violence against women: he'd assaulted his first wife, Kylie, and ignored an AVO she took out against him; assaulted his ex-fiancée and ignored her AVO; and in 1999 in Orange he'd held a woman against her will with such force she'd feared he would kill her.

Sussan Jean Kay had put her ordeal with Holdom behind her, but she'd been reminded when his face appeared on the front page of a newspaper in 2015. Now months later, she sat across from Detective Senior Constable Deon Kelly and recalled, in as much detail as she could despite the passage of time, her short-lived relationship with Holdom.

Holdom had been introduced to Sussan as 'Daniel Ford', in their hometown of Orange in the 1990s. Sussan, a polite, softly spoken woman of few words, had grown up in the quaint village of Millthorpe, twenty kilometres from Orange, before moving into town in her teens to attend high school.

It was late 1999 when she ran into the man she knew as Danny at Orange swimming pool. It was his dark, soulless eyes that jogged her memory. 'You never forget those eyes,' she would later recall.

That day, summer was still around the corner but the heat was fierce enough to pack the swimming pool. Sussan and Holdom had hit it off and spent the night together. She'd initially thought of it as a one-night stand, but Holdom was keen to see her again and soon was staying over at her house regularly.

At twenty-five years old, Sussan owned her own home, a large, single-level brick house on Sunset Place on the northern outskirts of town. Drying sheets and starched cloth nappies hung from a Hills hoist in the backyard and a tiny creek trickled behind the neat row of homes on the street. Sussan lived there with her nineteen-month-old son while her daughter stayed with her grandmother.

Holdom often came over unannounced but Sussan didn't mind; she liked how interested he seemed to be in her. Plus, he was kind to her son and often played with him on the lounge room floor while she fixed dinner in the kitchen.

But after a few weeks, Sussan began to see Holdom's interest as a mild obsession. He was intense and wanted to know where she was all the time, where she had been, and desperately pined for her affection. While Sussan liked the attention, she wasn't overly invested in the relationship. They hadn't shared a deep connection and their conversation consisted of mundane, day-to-day topics between watching late night videos and sex. There was no talk of Holdom's childhood or his future ambitions.

After a month, Sussan decided she didn't want to be with Holdom anymore. She left a handwritten note at her front door on 20 December 1999. It wasn't a long letter — no more than a dozen scribbled sentences on a piece of lined paper — but it laid out in plain English Sussan's grounds for wanting to break it off. She knew Holdom would come by at some point during the day and see the letter next to three empty bags he'd left at her house.

Anxious to avoid a confrontation, Sussan spent most of the day out of the house. But when she arrived home at about 5 pm with her tired son on her hip, she could see the bags and the letter were still on the front porch. Sighing, she went inside, wishfully thinking Holdom might get the picture and avoid knocking on her door.

She was wrong. Three hours later, Sussan found Holdom standing at the front door, scanning the letter as he tried to make sense of it all. He lifted his head and looked at her, confusion in his voice as he asked, almost begged, her to talk. He'd assumed their relationship was going along fine.

Reluctantly, Sussan opened the door. Even though she just wanted to put the short-lived relationship behind her, she felt sorry for Holdom and thought she better give him an opportunity to talk it over.

'Why are you doing this?' Holdom asked after plonking himself down on the couch. There was no aggression in his voice; he appeared rational and genuinely curious.

Sussan stated she simply wasn't satisfied with the relationship, that she needed more depth and engagement than he had been willing to give. Holdom's ego seemed bruised and Sussan sensed it; she tried to appease him, telling him they could still be friends.

The cliché offering was of some comfort to Holdom and he asked if he could stay a little while longer. Maybe they could watch a movie, he suggested. Sussan obliged.

At about 11 pm the video ended and Holdom continued his attempts to reconcile their broken relationship, but Sussan wasn't interested. She stood up and walked to her bedroom.

At 2 am Sussan rolled over in bed to find Holdom standing beside her. He said he was going home and Sussan, in her semi-awake state, nodded okay before turning over. She couldn't understand why he felt the need to wake her up to tell her that but she was too tired to care.

Suddenly, she felt a pillow pressing down on her face. She struggled to breathe as a paralysing fear rose up in her throat. Her arms flailed above her head and she felt Holdom's large strong hands pressing the pillow down with force.

'You have ruined my life,' Holdom said. He removed the pillow, locked his eyes on Sussan and wrapped both his hands around her throat; his thumbs dug into her skin and restricted her windpipe.

'Help me!' Sussan tried to scream, praying her neighbours would hear her.

As she lay there with Holdom's hands grasping her throat, her head felt foggy and her movements slowed as the energy powering her limbs depleted. If she couldn't get Holdom off her, he would surely kill her. She thought about her son asleep in the next room.

'Please, Danny, stop, you're hurting me,' Sussan pleaded. 'This won't end well for you. It'll get you nowhere. Please don't do this.'

Holdom's unblinking eyes suddenly flickered with recognition as his grip loosened a fraction, just enough for her to break free. Coughing and clutching at her throat, Sussan sobbed hysterically, overwhelmed with fear.

Holdom seemed like he was in a trance; he sat at the end of the bed and stared at his feet as Sussan shook uncontrollably and gulped air. She was desperate to get out of the room but she didn't want to antagonise him in case he tried to stop her.

'I promise I won't call the police, Danny,' she said in a despairing attempt to allay his concerns.

'You will,' Holdom snapped. 'You'll call the coppers and they'll press charges. I can't leave you here.'

Sussan changed tack; if it was the police Holdom was scared of, she would use that to get him out of her house.

'All right, if you don't leave I *will* call the police. They'll be over here in minutes and you'll be in handcuffs,' she warned, unsure if her strategy would work or make the situation worse.

The threat did the trick. A panicked Holdom sprinted from the house and down the street, disappearing into the night while Sussan crept into her son's bedroom. Tears streamed down her face, and she tried to compose herself as she looked down at her baby boy. He stirred in his cot, roused by the unfamiliar noises, but, most importantly, he was unharmed. Relieved, Sussan picked him up and held him. She brushed her hand through her hair and felt a thick clump of sticky material. It was two strips of grey duct tape from a roll she usually kept in her kitchen.

Horrified at the thought of Holdom's intention, she walked into the kitchen and found the cupboards wide open and the contents in disarray. With her son in her arms, she ran to her next door neighbour's house, banging on the door until someone appeared. Inconsolable, Sussan struggled to answer the neighbour's questions and only managed to ask him to call the police.

After that night, Sussan stayed at her mother's house, too frightened to return home in case Holdom found his way back. She never saw or heard from him again.

Holdom was eventually charged with ill treatment and common assault, minor charges that earned him a slap on the wrist and a $2000 fine in the Orange Local Court on 9 March 2001. The offence marked the first violent entry on Holdom's criminal record, which until that point was made up of disqualified driving charges.

There was a striking similarity between Holdom's assault on Sussan and the death of Khandalyce. Both had been suffocated and duct tape used in their terrifying ordeals.

Chapter 31

In a dark corner of a shed at Bishop's Lodge lay a pile of old bedspreads, the kind you'd expect to find at a country motel, with a pastel floral print that looked straight out of the 1980s. Detectives from Strike Force Malaya were discussing whether they should take the blankets away for forensic testing, in case they found traces of blood or other bodily fluids left behind by a crime committed eight years beforehand.

It was 11 November 2016, and a crime scene officer had already used Luminol, a solvent that illuminates blood traces, on the floors in Suite 32 and found no signs of blood. The bedspreads had been changed since 19 December 2008, when Holdom had checked in for two hours after he left Canberra with Khandalyce and before he turned up in Adelaide without her.

Something had happened in that ground level motel room on Larmer Street in Narrandera — a pleasant country location dubbed 'the town of trees', about an hour's drive west of Wagga — and police needed to find the evidence. It would be a time-consuming and arduous task, but perhaps examining the old musty bedspreads would pay off. Detectives were at the motel with a warrant granted by a Wagga Wagga magistrate after coming across a crucial piece of evidence that had narrowed their search for the location of Khandalyce's murder.

The month before, detectives had been tasked with retracing Holdom's ill-fated trips with Karlie to Belanglo State Forest and later with Khandalyce to Adelaide via southwest New South Wales. A study of Holdom's phone activity from December 2008 had allowed police to track his route, and a look at his bank transactions and credit card statements showed where he'd stopped along the way.

What detectives ended up with were two maps dotted with times and locations of where Holdom had made phone calls or sent text messages, using his phone and Karlie's, before and after each murder. Telecommunication companies stored metadata for seven years before it was destroyed, and the Strike Force Malaya request to access the records of Karlie and Holdom had fallen just within the retention period. Another two months and the records would have been deleted and crucial evidence lost forever.

After an analyst unscrambled the complex data — a mix of dates, times, locations and call durations — it came down to detectives to physically retrace Holdom's digital path.

They'd learned that at about 2:30 am on 15 December 2008, Holdom had left his cousin's home at Kerr Place in Charnwood. Based on statements from Christine and Dereck, police knew that he and Karlie were travelling in her Holden Commodore. Holdom's phone registered with the cell tower at Fraser as he headed northeast towards the Federal Highway, past Lake George and on to Goulburn. The 173-kilometre journey took two hours and twenty-one

minutes, with Holdom and Karlie reaching Belanglo State
Forest at about 4:51 am that morning.

Based on the phone data, Holdom stayed in the forest
for almost seven and a half hours until 12:16 pm. Judging by
the time stamps on the photographs, Holdom left the forest
about three-quarters of an hour after taking his last photo
of Karlie.

In June 2016, Detective Kelly and Detective Senior
Constable Victoria Lester stood at the intersection of the Red
Arm Creek Firetrail and the tiny, narrow unnamed track
where Karlie's bones had been found. It was serenely quiet,
if not for the crunch of brittle leaves underneath their boots.
It had been six years since dirt bike riders had uncovered
Karlie's skeleton, but instinctively the investigators looked
around for evidence or clues police officers before them may
have missed. While the fire trail felt lonely and isolated, it
was surprising how close Karlie's body had been dumped
to the edge of the forest. It didn't seem there had been a
concerted effort to hide her in the darkest depths of the
sprawling bushland; a car the size of Karlie's, a Holden
Commodore, could have easily fitted down the fire trail.

Detective Kelly, a quiet father-of-one with a forensic
mind who had been seconded to the strike force from the
Unsolved Homicide Team, had seen the photographs of
Karlie's body in this very spot.

After leaving the forest at about 12:16 pm, it appeared
Holdom used Karlie's phone to make calls or send messages
as he drove south along the Hume Highway, connecting
to phone towers named Freestone at 12:25 pm, Marulan
Plumb Hill at 12:50 pm and Mount Gray at 1:02 pm. The
phone data showed several minutes were spent in each area,
suggesting Holdom pulled over to make the calls.

At 1:46 pm he used his own phone around Lyneham, then he used Karlie's phone before swapping back to his own mobile as he passed the Bruce Stadium in the ACT. He reached Charnwood at about 2 pm.

Based on the statements from Christine and Dereck, when Holdom walked through the front door, he told the couple he'd had a fight with Karlie and taken her to a motel.

He said he would take Khandalyce back to her grandmother's house in South Australia and traded Karlie's car in for the white 1991 Holden Statesman.

In the early morning of 19 December 2008, with Khandalyce in a booster seat in the back of the Statesman, Holdom drove out of Charnwood and turned left on the Barton Highway. In daylight, the route through southwest New South Wales is picturesque, twisting through the Yass Valley's rolling, sheep-dotted hills and farmland of parched brown and vibrant green and gold. At night, the highway and everything around it is black, the only light source coming from passing headlights.

At 2:55 am Holdom's phone moved through Bookham, a tiny village in the Southern Tablelands known for a racetrack that inspired a Banjo Paterson poem. Four hours later he made a call near Coolac, a one-pub town not quite halfway between Sydney and Melbourne. A nonstop trip between those two country villages should only take thirty-five minutes, but Holdom's trip had taken four hours, based on his phone records.

There was little to see in the towns or on the route between them: kilometres of empty highway, countryside with jagged rocks and roaming cattle, and Jugiong, a town that skirts the Murrumbidgee River with an ageing motel and a petrol station. Forty minutes south of Bookham is the

Burrinjuck Dam, a holiday park on the river that was home to a small group of semi-permanent residents. Detectives pored over the records of everyone who lived around the dam but there was no reason for Holdom to go through there or anyone for him to visit.

By 8:16 am, Holdom had arrived in Wagga Wagga, New South Wales' largest inland city and the heart of the farming-rich Riverina region. He'd spent more than an hour in the regional hub and his credit card statement put him at the Woolworths supermarket at 8:48 am. In another case of record-keeping that worked in the detectives' favour, Woolworths, after a request to head office, was able to produce the receipt for Holdom's purchases.

Sighting the receipt was a jaw-dropping moment for the detectives. Holdom had purchased three Hercules garbage bags; one role of Home Handyman Duct Tape, 48 mm x 25 m; one litre of Coca-Cola; a 500 ml bottle of Palmolive Aromatherapy Anti-Stress Shower Gel; and a ten pack of DuraFresh Multi-purpose Wipes. The entire transaction cost $23.13, and the list of items seemed rudimentary enough but for the fact it was essentially a toolkit with which to murder Khandalyce.

The receipt became one of the final nails in Holdom's coffin. There could be no credible defence for Holdom purchasing the same silver duct tape — Woolworths had only ever stocked one type of silver duct tape — that had been found wrapped around Khandalyce's skull.

After making the incriminating purchases, Holdom had left Wagga Wagga at about 9:50 am and headed west. At 10:47 am, he arrived in Narrandera, Wagga's smaller and prettier cousin and a junction town where two major rural highways, the Newell and the Sturt, meet. During the day, the bulk of the town's activity buzzes around East Street. Larmer Street, the second street off the Sturt Highway at the entry into town from Wagga Wagga, is comparatively empty.

At 11:05 am, Holdom used his credit card, under the name Daniel Marshall, to pay $85 for a room at the Narrandera Midtown Motor Inn. The business had changed hands since, and on 1 October 2015 the new owners had renamed it Bishop's Lodge — ironically the same name as one of Holdom's aliases. Holdom had checked into Suite 32, a basic, one-bed room at the foot of the motel's steep driveway.

When detectives first arrived at the motel on 7 October 2016, the building had been painted and the rooms refurbished. The owners of the motel were more than happy to give the police access to their records. The detectives had two objectives in Narrandera: to find evidence that Holdom had been in town with Khandalyce, and to find the car seat she'd travelled in. While Holdom had left Charnwood with Khandalyce strapped into the seat, when he turned up in Adelaide the seat was nowhere to be seen, and it was assumed he'd gotten rid of it to hide evidence of his crime.

Throughout the four-hour drive from Canberra to Narrandera, Detective Kelly scanned the ditches next to the rural highway. He looked in bushes, culverts and on the roadsides in the tiny villages Holdom had stopped at. Behind the motel, he wandered down to Bundidgerry Creek, which twists around the southern boundary of Narrandera. It seemed like a fruitless task — what were the chances of finding the baby seat seven years after Holdom had passed through the town?

Back at the motel, detectives spent several hours sifting through a box of old check-in receipts, but there was no mention of Holdom. They needed to track down the previous managers, so they headed towards Wagga Wagga.

They made their way to a sprawling property on the southern outskirts of the town. Three dogs barked incessantly on the other side, so they stood at the front gate, not game enough to open it. They were there to speak to the former owner of the motel, Natalie Isaac, who had run the motel with her husband between 2008 and 2015.

When she emerged, the detectives told her they were investigating the murder of a mother and child and believed the killer stayed at her former business in 2008. Did she keep any of her records, including check-in slips or receipts from that time?

Mrs Isaac appeared apprehensive at first and initially told the investigators she didn't keep paperwork from that long ago. Detective Kelly's mind turned to the towel found in the suitcase with Khandalyce, which police had painstakingly been trying to track down. Actil, the manufacturer of the elderberry 'Down Under Towel' had provided South Australia Police with the batch number that matched the towel found with Khandalyce. Investigators had tried dozens of different places all over South Australia in an attempt to find a motel that stocked the same batch of towels but had been unsuccessful.

On a whim, Detective Kelly asked Mrs Isaac if she remembered using the elderberry towels in the motel when she worked there.

'I use one to wash the dogs,' she told the detective matter-of-factly before producing a towel from her house.

Detective Kelly examined the towel. The batch number matched the batch number of the towel found in the suitcase. All the evidence was pointing to Khandalyce being killed in Narrandera.

However, while detectives were able to confirm the origin of the towel, they didn't get the guest check-in document they were after.

Mrs Isaac seemed shaken by her unwitting involvement in the murder investigation. When approached for this book in December 2018, Mrs Isaac was polite but reluctant to talk. She seemed haunted by what had occurred and didn't want to revisit the past. Mrs Isaac said she wished she could have done something to change what happened in Suite 32.

Undeterred, Detective Kelly kept in contact with Mrs Isaac over the following days, just in case she stumbled across something useful. Almost two weeks later, on 10 October 2016, after the detectives returned to Sydney, his phone rang. It was Mrs Isaac. She'd gone through her old files and thought she'd found what they were looking for.

An urgent request was made to Wagga Wagga detectives to go around to Mrs Isaac's place as soon as possible to get the document. When it finally reached the Homicide Squad, it had more significance than the investigators had anticipated.

The guest registration was handwritten and included the following details: Daniel Marshall; 12 Kerr Place Charnwood; YZT 444; $85 paid; Suite No: 32; Adults: 1, Children: 1.

Holdom had spent his life lying to wriggle out of difficult situations but in this instance he told the truth, confirming he'd checked into the motel with a child, and it would be his undoing.

It was the last record of Khandalyce alive.

Despite the passage of time, Holdom's fingerprint was recovered from the document, and the handwriting compared against other documents with his handwriting. Both provided very strong support that Holdom had signed the guest registration.

The following month, police returned to the motel with a warrant in the hope of uncovering evidence that would prove Khandalyce was killed inside Suite 32. But they could find nothing in the room and after some discussion, they decided that forensic testing of every single bedspread at the motel would not be a worthwhile use of time and resources.

However, both the towel and the guest registration placed Khandalyce at the motel before Holdom continued his journey on 19 December 2008. At 1:20 pm that day, Holdom left Narrandera and his phone bounced off cell towers in Hay, Mildura, Renmark and Loxton as he made his way across first the New South Wales border into Victoria and then the Victorian border into South Australia.

Around midnight, he was in the vicinity of the Karoonda Exchange cell tower for twenty-five minutes, and at 12:52 am on 20 December, his mobile phone was recorded at a town near Murray Bridge. The main route connecting those two towns in the Murray Mallee was the Karoonda Highway — the empty stretch where the suitcase containing Khandalyce's bones had been found.

At 2:06 am on 20 December 2008, twenty-four hours after he'd left Canberra, Holdom arrived at Hazel's house in Adelaide, where his cold dinner waited on the table.

Khandalyce was not with him.

Chapter 32

21 August 2017

His face had been splashed all over the news but, until today, Daniel Holdom had been an enigma. He was a high-profile criminal who's life had been dissected in news reports but he had not been seen in the flesh.

Now, for the first time, almost two years after he was charged, Holdom was finally fronting court in person rather than hiding behind an audio-visual link-up from Goulburn jail.

The day marked the start of his committal hearing, but the wheels of justice were moving painfully slowly. Holdom had been trying every delay tactic he could. He'd even suggested his life would be in danger if he had to appear in court in person.

Less than three weeks earlier, on 1 August 2017, Holdom had unexpectedly announced that he'd sacked his legal team. 'I wasn't getting the right advice,' he told Magistrate Les Mabbutt. 'I am applying for a private solicitor and for legal aid to pay for it.'

Sure enough, while Prosecutor Victoria Engel was standing at the far right side of the bar table, the other end — usually occupied by a defence lawyer — was empty.

Holdom's last-minute ditching of his legal team had presented a conundrum — a new lawyer would not be able to read the entire brief of evidence in time for the committal hearing.

Claiming he hadn't seen all the information in the 42-volume brief of evidence, Holdom had then asked for a two-month adjournment so he could read all the material.

But Magistrate Mabbutt wasn't having his scheduled hearing derailed. 'These are two charges of murder, Mr Holdom, that have been in the courts for two years,' he said, peering over his glasses. As the presiding magistrate at Sydney's busiest local court, Mabbutt took a swift approach to dealing with the dozens of cases that crossed his bench every day. Hearing dates in the judicial system were precious; some cases waited months before they could secure a hearing before a magistrate or a judge in the district court.

Holdom put his head in his hands, visibly frustrated that things weren't going his way. But Magistrate Mabbutt said he would not cancel or vacate the hearing dates. 'I will hear further from you in a week or so,' he said.

Now, three weeks on, as Holdom sat in the dock of courtroom four at Sydney's Central Local Court for the committal hearing, he looked anxious and frail, which seemed at odds with the brutality of his crimes. It showed him in a new light — irritable, scared and stressed. The enormity of the police case against him was about to be laid bare, and it appeared to be weighing heavily on him.

Journalists and Strike Force Malaya detectives had packed the rear of the courtroom; Karlie's aunt and uncle, Ray and Nick Bell, were also there.

Nick glared at Holdom and made a subtle but threatening gesture that only Holdom witnessed.

Holdom whispered to a young solicitor who was now occupying the defence end of the bar table. Edward Chee had been to Goulburn jail to visit Holdom, with fellow solicitor Jeannette Fahd, and was waiting on Holdom's legal aid grant to be approved before his firm officially acted for him. Sensing the magistrate's reluctance to adjourn the committal hearing, Mr Chee had attended as *amicus curiae* — 'a friend of the court' who offered information or assistance during a case but wasn't technically representing a client. Next to the DPP solicitors with their trolleys packed with bursting, legal arch folders, Mr Chee's single pad of blank A4 paper and pen looked painfully underprepared.

After talking to Holdom through a narrow gap in the glass-walled dock, Mr Chee got to his feet. 'A member of the public gallery has on two occasions made gestures to Mr Holdom,' he said to the magistrate.

Mabbutt glanced towards the back of the court. 'If anyone interferes with [the hearing] I'll have them removed from the courtroom,' he said before starting the proceedings.

In another attempt to stop the hearing, Holdom revealed he had left some of his brief of evidence in Goulburn jail. If the evidence was going to be referred to throughout the hearing, Holdom would need his copy to follow what was going on.

The revelation prompted incredulous sighs from the public gallery. Holdom then claimed he had only received thirty volumes of the brief of evidence, but his former lawyer, when contacted by the DPP, confirmed he'd in fact received all of it. The case was adjourned again.

The next day, as Magistrate Mabbutt walked into the courtroom, he was told Holdom had been admitted to hospital the night before and hadn't been able to get his brief from Goulburn. Holdom had recovered remarkably from his short stint in hospital and was seated in the dock again. Ever determined, Mabbutt asked one of two guards seated next to Holdom if someone could go into Holdom's cell, get the tubs containing his legal documents, put them on a prison truck and bring them to the court.

With a quick bow, the officer scurried downstairs to make a phone call. He returned with bad news: Corrective Services only made twice-weekly trips transporting prisoners between Goulburn and Sydney. Holdom's brief could be picked up but it wouldn't arrive for a few days.

Mabbutt's patience was running thin and he turned to stare at Holdom. The hearing couldn't go ahead if Holdom's prospective lawyer, who was masking any shared frustration very well, wasn't aware of all the evidence against Holdom. It would shape any legal advice he provided to Holdom. But as he wasn't officially assigned as Holdom's lawyer yet, Mr Chee hadn't yet received his own copy of the brief of evidence.

The voluminous brief was made up of thousands of pages of witness statements, interview transcripts, forensic reports and photographs that would take a lot of time and money to copy. In the interests of time, Mabbutt asked for a digital copy of the brief of evidence that he could read while Holdom read his hard copy. In a continuing litany of delays that would have bordered on comical if not for the extremely serious nature of the case, the digital copy was on a CD; the magistrate's laptop only had USB ports, not a disk drive.

The magistrate asked whether Holdom could be provided with a laptop to read the digital brief.

However, it turned out Corrective Services could only allow Holdom access to a computer for an hour because of restrictions placed on his classification as an inmate. There was little choice but to adjourn the hearing for a few days, much to the disappointment of Ray and Nick, who had to return to Adelaide for work and would miss the bulk of the hearing. The prosecutor, Ms Engel, tended the voluminous brief of evidence — which occupied its own office in the DPP building — for the magistrate to read and assess the evidence independently.

Over the next two days, Holdom's brief was collected from his cell in Goulburn and delivered to the courthouse. Mabbutt closed the court so Holdom and Mr Chee could go through the material, folder by folder.

It was decided the hearing would be a paper committal: there would be no witnesses called to give evidence in court. The magistrate would simply read all the evidence and make a decision on whether the case should progress to a higher court.

Finally, after Mr Mabbutt spent two days poring over thousands of pages, including 'sensitive material' — the images of Karlie's naked body inside a sealed envelope — he returned to the bench in Central Local Court on 24 August to hand down his decision.

First, Ms Engel read out the Crown case statement onto the public record. The public had heard about the fraud carried out in Karlie's name after her death, the use of her mobile phone to create the illusion she was alive, and where the bodies of her and her daughter were found.

But that was only a quarter of the evidence. Few people knew about how the mother and daughter had been killed, the measures Holdom had taken to keep his secret, and the crucial pieces of evidence that connected him to the murders.

A collective silence swept across the courtroom and people seated in the public gallery leaned forward to hear Ms Engel's address. Poor acoustics in the dated courtroom made the situation challenging, however, the weight of her submissions was heard loud and clear.

Karlie's ribs had been cracked, an injury likely caused by being stomped on. Holdom had taken 'trophy' photographs of her body and had subjected her to sexual assault after she'd died.

'The evidence, including photographing her body in situ, as a trophy of sorts, is indicative of an intention to kill,' Ms Engel said.

Motivated by a sexual desire for children, Holdom had then returned to the ACT for her daughter. Holdom had bought duct tape and dishcloths at Wagga Wagga Woolworths before he checked into a motel and signed himself and a child into Suite 32. Khandalyce's skull still had duct tape stretched across it and balls of dishcloth were stuffed in her mouth when her bones were finally found in July 2015.

The totality of the evidence was overwhelming and chilling. Journalists glanced at each other with open mouths, shocked at the revelations.

Before Ms Engel sat down, she asked the court to put in place a suite of non-publication orders that would prohibit the media publishing several key details: the names of Dereck

Dover, Hazel Passmore, Toni Blundell, Christine Lancaster, the duct tape and dishcloths found with Khandalyce's bones, and the sexual nature of both crimes. With a trial still months away, the prosecution wanted to protect the safety of the witnesses and the dignity of Karlie and Khandalyce.

With his chin placed on his left hand and elbow resting on a narrow timber bench, Holdom seemed tense and uncomfortable, as if everyone judging him from the public gallery would interpret any move he made.

Magistrate Mabbutt began to deliver his reasons for why he found there was an overwhelming circumstantial case against Holdom.

'Karlie and the accused were both staying at an address with the offender's relatives,' he said. 'Statements from Lancaster and Dover are that the accused had an argument with Karlie, and on 14 December 2008 they left the house in Karlie's Holden Commodore station wagon.

'Khandalyce remained with Lancaster and Dover, and the accused was gone for fourteen to seventeen hours. He returned the next day. Dover was asked to clean the car; Karlie didn't return with the accused.'

Mabbutt continued with his summary of the evidence. Dereck said Holdom had a scratch on his face and removed a blanket from Karlie's car. Holdom told Dereck he'd had an argument with Karlie and dropped her at a bus stop. Four days later, on 19 December 2008, Holdom left with Khandalyce and travelled to South Australia.

'The prosecution says those two dates are the last dates there has been any confirmed sighting of Khandalyce or her mother, Karlie,' Mabbutt said.

He went through the use of Karlie's bank account, the missing person's report, the use of Karlie's mobile phone to provide her mother with false hope that she'd return to Alice Springs.

'Of course Karlie and her daughter didn't come home,' he said.

There were the statements from Holdom's ex-girlfriends, including Toni (who claimed she couldn't remember writing the diary entry about Holdom's confession), the inconsistencies in his police interviews and the images.

'The nexus between the accused, the SD card, how it came into the possession of Hazel Passmore and how police got it, are all compelling factors in respect of the probity value of the photos,' Mabbutt said. 'They are graphic images.'

The case was a 'large and complex' circumstantial case and there was nothing in the photographs to suggest there was more than one offender involved. The Crown submitted the motive to kill Karlie was to get access to her child and that Holdom sexually assaulted the toddler — crimes that involved premeditation and planning.

'I am satisfied on both charges the prosecution case is capable of satisfying a jury properly instructed that the accused murdered Khandalyce and Karlie,' Magistrate Mabbutt said. 'Stand up, Mr Holdom. Do you wish to say anything in relation to the charges?'

Holdom slowly stood and folded his arms, his hands hidden under his armpits. 'No, Your Honour,' he replied with a shake of his head.

Holdom was committed to stand trial in the New South Wales Supreme Court. On 2 February 2018, he would plead not guilty to two counts of murder.

Part IV

Justice

Justice

Chapter 33

31 July 2018

Winter was bitterly cold in Queen's Square. The few rays of sunlight that warmed the courtyard in the centre of Sydney's justice precinct did not emerge until lunchtime, when solicitors and judges' associates streamed out of chambers to tuck into their packed lunches on park benches. A line of suits snaked out of Jardin, a French-themed cafe in the southern pocket of the square, a few metres from the top of the stairs to St James train station.

Squeezed in between the legal hub of Phillip Street and Macquarie Street, the home of New South Wales Parliament House, Queen's Square is a mix of old and new. In one corner is the King Street court complex — its marble floors, creaking spiral staircase and ruby-red carpet are full of character and history. Sydney's notorious criminals had learned their fate in the docks of those courtrooms and the portraits of great legal minds hung on the walls.

Across the square is the modern but unoriginally named Law Courts Building, an unremarkable tower with tall glass windows on the ground floor that is more attractive inside than out. There are no initials or crass words carved out of the wooden benches in the public gallery of its neat courtrooms, where everything appears orderly and civilised.

On level 11 of the Law Courts Building, in courtroom 11C, Detective Gunn, Detective Senior Constable Brenton Sommerville, the second in charge of Strike Force Malaya, and Detective Senior Constable Benjamin Morgan sat in the front row in the left-hand corner of the public gallery, not far from the prosecutor at the bar table. It was an unusually busy day for courts in Sydney and there was a familiar name on the Supreme Court list that morning — Daniel James Holdom.

Holdom's appearance in court was unexpected, so much so that most of Sydney's court reporters, bar the *Daily Telegraph*'s Emma Partridge, were absent.

In seven days' time, Holdom's mammoth double murder trial was due to begin, nine years and eight months after Karlie and Khandalyce had been killed. Of the 381 witnesses in the case, 182 had been served with subpoenas to give evidence at the trial. Travel arrangements were being made. Witnesses had sought time off from their respective jobs.

The evidence implicating Holdom in the murders was overwhelming but he had refused to budge or admit guilt.

Under New South Wales sentencing laws, offenders can receive a 25 per cent discount on their sentence for entering a plea at the earliest opportunity. Further discounts are warranted if the criminal assists police, but the percentage starts to shrink the longer the offender drags the case through the courts. The incentive is meant to encourage criminals to admit to their crimes sooner rather than later, even if that means striking a deal with the DPP to drop the most serious charge in return for a guilty plea to a lesser offence. It saves the court time in an age when the waiting period for a trial date can be more than twelve months, and saves victims' families the anguish of reliving the trauma in minute detail.

At 9 am on the dot, Justice Robert Allan Hulme walked into the courtroom and took a seat at the bench.

Crown prosecutor Mark Tedeschi QC — who had recently retired from the DPP but had returned to run the Holdom case — and defence barrister Greg Woods QC announced their appearances as the court transcribers recorded every word.

'If Your Honour pleases, I present an indictment against the accused,' Mr Tedeschi said.

'Please stand, Mr Holdom,' Justice Hulme said.

The judge's associate, seated directly below the bench and dressed in black robes, cleared her throat and stood up to read out the indictment.

'For that he, between 13 December 2008 and 16 December 2008 at Belanglo or elsewhere in the state of New South Wales, did murder Karlie Jade Pearce-Stevenson.'

'Guilty,' Holdom replied in a deep hoarse voice, his eyes locked on the front of the courtroom.

'Further that he, between 18 December 2008 and 21 December 2008 at Narrandera or elsewhere in the state of New South Wales, did murder Khandalyce Kiara Pearce.'

'Guilty.'

With that, the prospect of a twelve-week trial was waived and Holdom's three years of denying guilt came to a swift end. There were no elated cheers or tears of relief from the public gallery; hardly anyone outside the defence and prosecution teams knew the plea of guilty was coming. The change of tack came as a surprise to the detectives, who had been working on evidence to be presented at trial right up until the last moment.

Mr Tedeschi offered to hand the judge an outline of the prosecution case, the statement of facts, but Justice Hulme wouldn't have it. The defence and the Crown were still negotiating the finer details of what Holdom had admitted to, and it would be amended at a sentence hearing on 28 September.

'I don't want to receive anything that's not in final form. It will only confuse me potentially,' Hulme said.

The case was adjourned and everyone in the courtroom stood while Justice Hulme turned to the right and exited. Holdom raised his bandaged left hand and whispered, 'Thank you,' before Corrective Services officers escorted him out of the dock. It seemed like a very relaxed affair for such a momentous development.

The detectives walked outside the courtroom into the quiet hallway on level 11, and shook hands with the prosecution team. Away from the formalities of the court, the mood was a mix of jubilation and relief. Detective Gunn peeled off from the group to call NSW Homicide Squad boss Detective Superintendent Scott Cook, who had been appointed in late 2017, and relayed the good news.

He then called Bruce Pearce and Scott Povey.

'It's a good outcome guys,' Detective Gunn told the men. 'The indictment has been read out in court, it's all formal now so you can tell anyone you want.'

The detectives and Ms Engel caught the lift to the bottom floor of the Law Courts Building, walked out the glass bi-fold doors and quietly celebrated with a coffee at the quaint cafe in the corner of the cold Queen's Square.

Chapter 34

With his left hand still wrapped in a bandage, Holdom flicked through three pages in a plastic-sleeve folder resting on a narrow bench inside the dock. He'd taken one quick glance at the relatives of his victims seated in the first two rows inside courtroom 13A and dared not look back. He appeared caught off guard by the vast number of family members who had travelled great distances to face him at his sentencing hearing in Sydney.

In a show of unity, they'd filed into the modern courtroom inside the Law Courts Building, minutes before the hearing was about to start. Quietly showing them to their seats was Detective Senior Constable Brenton Sommerville. The case was the first Sommerville had been assigned to after he joined the Homicide Squad in 2016 and he'd quickly come to know the investigation inside and out. To some he was a familiar face.

Justice Robert Allan Hulme walked in and sat at the bench. It had been two months since he'd accepted Holdom's two guilty pleas and he was about to hear submissions

from both the prosecution and the defence on what an
appropriate penalty should be. In the Crown's view, nothing
less than life in prison would suffice, a submission Karlie and
Khandalyce's family strongly supported.

On a television screen above Holdom's head were the
faces of Bruce Pearce and Scott Povey, who would watch
the hearing via audio-visual links from Port Augusta
and Darwin respectively. On Mr Pearce's arms are two
tattoos — his first and only — of Karlie and Khandalyce,
vivid reminders of love and loss.

The connection on Scott's end was poor and it was
difficult to hear what was going on inside the New South
Wales Supreme Court. At his request, a cloth had also been
placed over the camera transmitting images from Scott's
end to the Sydney courtroom to ensure Holdom couldn't
see him. Scott didn't want the man responsible for his grief
drawing any satisfaction from his reactions.

For several weeks, Scott had been crafting his victim
impact statement, a document he'd poured his emotional
turmoil and darkest moments into. He'd managed to reduce
the statement from thirty pages to six, but was hesitant to
have it read out in court at all. There was no way Scott, a
deeply genuine but very private man, was going to read it
out himself either. After the breakthrough in Karlie's and
Khandalyce's cases became nationwide news in 2015, he'd
knocked back request after request for media interviews
without a second thought. He wanted to grieve in private
and resented the endless calls to his mobile phone from
reporters.

He respected the police had a job to do, even though
it had meant keeping a secret from those closest to him,
and in turn they respected him. Scott was told of major

developments in the case before they were publicised — the identification of Karlie and Khandalyce, Holdom's imminent guilty plea — because detectives trusted he wouldn't tell anyone.

Unwittingly and undeservedly, Scott had found himself in a traumatic situation with repercussions that were completely foreign to him. When he walked down the street, he felt like people recognised him as the father of a murder victim and he was racked by such anxiety that he'd retreated for months and barely spoke to anyone. He'd sought support from the South Australia Victims' Rights Commissioner Michael O'Connell to deal with his grief, the public attention, and the drafting of written public statements to placate the media interest.

In the lead-up to the sentencing hearing, he'd told Ms Engel he didn't want the contents of his statement placed on the public record; truth was, he didn't want Holdom to hear the personal pain he had put to paper. Victim impact statements are voluntary; family members of victims or victims themselves can choose to prepare one after an offender is convicted. It provides an opportunity for them to play a part in the justice system, a world that often seems intimidating and overwhelming. A judge takes into account the victims' views, but does not draw any conclusions if they opt not to prepare a statement.

On the off-chance Scott had a change of mind, Ms Engel called him on the morning of the hearing and asked him one last time if he was sure he didn't want his words read out, even by someone on his behalf. Surprisingly, he *had* had a change of heart and agreed to South Australia victim support officer Debbie Gibson reading out his statement for him. Ms Gibson had come to know Scott and his family well over the past three years, having been appointed by South Australia's Major Crime Investigation Branch to provide support and explain the complexities and formalities of the judicial system.

It takes a rare degree of resilience and empathy to be a homicide victim support person. They willingly walk a stranger's path of grief and are available 24/7 in a taxing but rewarding role that often leads to lifelong friendships. At a small service in Adelaide, where Khandalyce's remains were repatriated from South Australia to Alice Springs to be met with Karlie's remains ahead of the funeral in December 2015, Ms Gibson was a pallbearer. She had gone above and beyond in her support and Scott held her in the highest esteem. Without her, Scott doubted he would have coped.

It would be the first time he had publicly detailed the difficulties he had faced over the past decade and he trusted Ms Gibson would deliver it justly. With Scott's printed statement in her hand, Ms Gibson sat down in the witness box and leaned towards the microphone.

'My heart was ripped out of me and my soul torn from my existence when I was told by detectives that the little girl found dumped in a suitcase, the story that I had been reading and seeing on the news, was Khandalyce, my granddaughter,' she said on Scott's behalf.

'I knew then Karlie was dead. The worst nightmare imaginable itself will not explain how I felt. I could not hug Karlie's mum. I could not talk to friends, I could not even scream at the world. I could not talk at all, and once again I had to hold onto another secret, kept from those closest while detectives searched for Karlie.'

Scott had pushed his family away and created barriers between himself and new friends so they wouldn't put two and two together. Life had been a blur, one day rolling into the next without distinction and Scott had merely existed. His saving grace was his partner, Brenda, an 'unbelievably strong woman' who had been unintentionally dragged into his past and forced to grapple with the grief.

Karlie had made a decision many young women did — to leave her hometown, move away from family and friends and experience a new environment, but she was robbed of the option to come back and to realise that path wasn't for her.

'Karlie never had her opportunity to change her path that all of us have travelled when young, to make the decision and say "this is not what I want" and head in another direction.'

There was nothing Scott could have done to stop the murders but, like Bruce, he analysed in torturous detail the 'what ifs'.

'Although I have been told many times that this is not my fault, that this was out of my control, that there is absolutely nothing I could have done,' he wrote, 'I feel that I have failed the very fundamental essence of family, that I could not protect, shield or divert Karlie from her demise and keep her daughter safe and close to my wife.

'With an unreligious redemption, I live with this like a journey to hell and only halfway back, and unwillingly, I have taken others with me.'

One relative seated in court held her head in her hands; her grey hair covered her face and shielded her tears.

'Today Karlie should have been thirty years old and Khandalyce twelve, preparing to start high school next year,' Scott wrote.

A father's guilt and remorse were laid bare. 'I am sorry, Karlie, for being angry because you wouldn't talk to your mum for so long. I am sorry that I blamed you for your mum's sadness and for being angry when you didn't come to say goodbye to your mum. We didn't know you couldn't. I know now that I will never see you to say I'm sorry.

'I felt something was wrong that morning, Karlie. I told your mum to ring you because I knew you were in trouble. You were so far away, and we did not know where you were, and you did not answer. I now know you couldn't.'

Ms Gibson stepped out of the witness box and walked back to her seat as the stinging sadness of Scott's words hung in the air. It was impossible not to be moved by the father's raw and confronting words. The hearing was about Holdom's cruel and fatal crimes, but at the heart of the case was a family who had lost two people they cherished and had been taunted by the unknown for a decade.

Across the room, Holdom looked preoccupied with his documents. At times he appeared bored, his head rested in the palm of his hand, or uncomfortable as he squirmed in his chair.

Karlie's aunty, Kellie Lilly, read out the statement prepared by Bruce Pearce.

'The anger, the pain and the hurt that entered my life on 15 October 2015, when I found out that Karlie and Khandalyce had been so brutally murdered, has changed my life forever,' she said on his behalf. 'The anger, the pain and the hurt never goes away. The unanswered questions haunt me daily.'

Holdom continued to mindlessly fidget with the papers in front of him, seeming unsure of where to look.

'The hate that I feel is consuming. I have never hated anyone the way that I hate you,' Ms Lilly went on. 'You have taken my daughter and granddaughter from our family. You have taken away a granddaughter that I never got to meet.

I would always think about meeting Khandalyce and seeing Karlie. My thoughts were that she was off in the world living her life and she will come back when she was ready to settle down.'

Bruce had worked in the mines up until October 2015, but the anger he felt after finding out about the murders had impacted on his ability to engage with his colleagues and control his emotions. He moved back to Port Augusta, where his days were spent at the shacks, reminiscing about holidays spent at the same spot teaching Karlie how to fish and catch crabs. Sleepless nights tormented him, as did the questions about his daughter's and granddaughter's suffering.

Mr Pearce wondered if he could have stopped the mother and child going to Canberra with Holdom, if only he'd been in Port Augusta when they'd passed through in late 2008.

'At first I had a feeling of guilt. How could I have protected her?' Mr Pearce's statement read. 'If I was at Mum's house when you were there, would I have been able to keep them here to protect them? Would they have stayed for longer? Could I have saved both their lives? Could I have made a difference?' No punishment would ease the pain or suffering of his family; even the death penalty would not suffice.

Ms Lilly walked back to the public gallery and a relative placed a consoling arm around her shoulders. Another whispered that she'd done well.

Karlie's uncle Allan Brookes was next to read out a statement on behalf of Karlie's grandmother and Khandalyce's great-grandmother, Lorna Pearce. Mrs Pearce reflected on seeing Karlie for the last time, when she and Khandalyce stopped at her house in Port Augusta on the way south in late 2008. She had been ecstatic to see them but the mood changed when Holdom walked in the front door after the mother and child.

'There was no enjoyment at seeing him,' Mr Brookes said on her behalf. 'Since that time I have watched my family suffer from what you have taken from us by the terrible acts you have committed.

'My time with my beautiful granddaughters was cut short in seeing them again and never seeing them achieve milestones in life. I still have trouble sleeping and cry often [for] my beautiful granddaughters and I wish I had stopped them from leaving.' Watching her son, Bruce, racked by grief was difficult to grasp.

Mr Brookes walked back to his seat and sat next to his partner, who clenched a tissue in her right hand.

Emotions were running high and Justice Hulme, in his heavy red and gold robes, thanked the family for their courage.

'Mr Pearce and Mr Povey, I thank you for putting down on paper the description of the terrible impact this crime has had on you, and the offender gets to hear as well,' he said.

The Crown prosecutor, Mark Tedeschi QC, rose from his seat and placed his submissions on the timber lectern before him. Mr Tedeschi was a master of the courtroom, one of the state's most experienced and highly respected prosecutors who had spent forty-one years at the bar and thirty-five years as a Crown prosecutor.

He'd been appointed to the Holdom case late in the piece and was guided by Ms Engel, who had carried the case from charge to sentence. Her attention to detail and forensic mind made her a very good lawyer. But it was the compassion and empathy she showed to victims and their families that made her a brilliant prosecutor.

At the sentencing hearing she was seated at the bar table in black robes and a barrister's wig, a sign of her recent ascension to the role of Crown prosecutor. She was one of the youngest Crown prosecutors appointed in New South Wales' history.

Sporadically, Ms Engel passed Mr Tedeschi notes or answered his whispered questions while he was on his feet addressing the judge. He meticulously detailed the facts of each murder, from Karlie's death in the Belanglo State Forest — 'the last moments of Karlie's life must have been horrendous for her' — to the photographs of her body.

'She was isolated in the forest, she was far from her young daughter,' Mr Tedeschi said. 'She was murdered by a man whom she had been in a relationship with.'

He revealed another gotcha moment: a mole on Holdom's arm had been matched to a mole on the arm captured in one of the photographs with Karlie's naked body.

Karlie's murder had been motivated by a number of factors, including the intent to gain access to her young daughter, who Holdom had expressed a sexual interest in, and financial gain. 'The offender engaged in long-term, sophisticated fraud, including obtaining welfare benefits.'

Hazel's pending law suit against Holdom over the car crash could also be seen as a motive. He was about to encounter money troubles as a result of being sued, and stealing money from Karlie after her death would help lessen the blow, Mr Tedeschi argued.

The fraud committed in Karlie's name was a continuation of Holdom's reputation as a fraudster. He had convictions for more than twenty fraud offences between 2003 and 2013, and it showed he felt no remorse for the murders he'd committed.

There was also a sexual motive. It was a thrill kill, Mr Tedeschi said, as was evidenced by the trophy photographs Holdom took and kept for years. He was a 'man of extreme dangerousness' and 'devoid of care or empathy'. Her murder must have involved a protracted case of violence and gratuitous cruelty.

The last moment of Khandalyce's life must have been equally horrific Mr Tedeschi said. It was highly likely she was trussed up with dishcloths shoved in her mouth and duct tape across it when she was still alive, so Holdom could sexually abuse her.

Due to the deterioration of Khandalyce's remains, police would never know whether she had actually been sexually assaulted or to what extent, but given Holdom's well-documented interest in children, it was likely he'd planned on it.

'He could never after the sexual assault, allow her to live,' Mr Tedeschi said. 'There was a level of planning involved, having murdered Karlie and disposed of her car and having made plans to go to South Australia. He must have taken the child away with the idea in mind that he was going to murder her.'

Both murders fell within the worst category and could only be described as atrocious, extremely wicked and reprehensible. His guilty pleas were merely an acknowledgement of an 'inevitable conviction'.

* * *

'This man is not psychotic, this man is not a psychopath.'

Defence barrister Greg Woods QC, a former district court judge with a wealth of legal experience, was on his feet putting forward Holdom's subjective circumstances in a bid to explain why his client was the way he was.

It was a difficult task; Holdom had pleaded guilty a week out from trial, showed little remorse, and had made no attempt to answer the question at the centre of every murder case: Why?

Even Dr Woods' attempt at an apology on behalf of his client received a shaky reception.

'As counsel for Holdom, I wish to put on the record in front of some of the victims' relatives his apology to them and the court for the grave crimes he has committed and to which he confessed when he pleaded guilty,' Dr Woods said as Holdom stared blank-faced at the judge.

'I'll have to think whether I give that any weight at all,' Justice Hulme swiftly replied.

It was an apology on instructions from Holdom's lawyer and it didn't amount to remorse. Known among his colleagues for his unrivalled ability to recall obscure sections of law from the deepest corners of criminal legislation, Justice Hulme knew both sides of the bar well. He'd been a deputy senior Crown prosecutor and had acted as Mr Tedeschi's junior barrister in the trial of Phuong Ngo, who was convicted of murdering New South Wales MP John Newman in 1994, and he'd been a public defender. On the bench he was patient and efficient but clearly had low tolerance for insincerity.

Seated next to Dr Woods was Holdom's solicitor, Jeannette Fahd. She was furiously taking notes between responding to questions from Holdom. He'd discreetly wave his bandaged hand in her direction when he had something to say. At times he looked incredulous at what Mr Tedeschi was submitting about his actions and would shake his head in disagreement.

Ms Fahd, her dark hair pulled back in a tight, low bun, would walk over to the dock and listen to his queries. She'd give him a patient nod, a reassuring word and return to her chair to guide Dr Woods through submissions that relied heavily on Holdom's disadvantaged upbringing.

Using an approach in his submissions that Holdom had tested in court before, Dr Woods said that while his client committed the murders of Karlie and Khandalyce in 2008, his story began in 1974. From birth, Holdom had a very disordered and abusive childhood that was 'causative of the offences before the court'.

'Though he has done dreadful things to which he has pleaded guilty, dreadful things were done to him,' Dr Woods said, pausing briefly to adjust his robes.

The systemic abuse — throwing of boiling water on Holdom as a child, long periods without food, lack of love from his mother and overwhelming disdain displayed by his stepfather — was relevant. If he had been brought up in a supportive household, it was highly unlikely Holdom would have killed Karlie and Khandalyce, Dr Woods argued cautiously.

Holdom didn't know why he'd committed the murders because he'd had such a shocking childhood and it had distorted the rest of his life. While he had been 'very troublesome' and a criminal, he lacked the element that justified permanently locking him up for life, Dr Woods submitted. He referred to the offences as 'crimes of uncontrolled passion', a submission that almost earned a scoff from Justice Hulme, who was 'not sure that was an apt description'.

Dr Woods elaborated: Hazel claimed Holdom killed Karlie 'for her' so they could rekindle their volatile relationship, and then murdered Khandalyce because her mere presence would have raised suspicion.

Holdom had pleaded guilty to the murders and agreed to the Crown's version of how the killings played out, contained in the statement of facts. He'd dug his heels in on pleading guilty until the eleventh hour and had agonised over details in the police allegations that he didn't agree with. Holdom's reason for murdering Karlie and Khandalyce had not been detailed, or at least their family had not heard his explanation.

Ms Fahd had requested a psychiatric report from Dr Olav Nielssen, who had interviewed Holdom from Goulburn Correctional Centre on 8 August 2018. During the interview, Holdom spoke about the 2008 fatal car crash, his descent into heavy drug use, two suicide attempts in jail, his history of failed relationships and his troublesome upbringing.

While providing an opinion of Holdom's state of mind and mental state, Dr Nielssen got as close as anyone to extracting a reason from Holdom as to why he did what he admitted to doing. It was hard to know what to believe, given Holdom's habit of lying, but the flippant and vague language he used to explain the killings was undeniably disturbing.

Justice Hulme read out a small part of Holdom's interview, in which he admitted to killing Khandalyce, detailed in Dr Nielssen's report.

'It is horrible I guess, she got suffocated,' Holdom told the psychiatrist. 'Not turning up with her mum would have raised questions about why she wasn't with her.'

Holdom claimed he killed the child while he was in Canberra and took her dead body in the car as he drove to Adelaide, dumping her in the suitcase on the way. It contradicted evidence and didn't explain how Holdom checked into the Narrandera motel with one child on 19 December 2008.

Family members in the public gallery shook their heads and glared at Holdom, who dared not meet their stares, while Justice Hulme described Holdom's explanation as lacking in detail and unhelpful.

In further details that were not read out in court, Holdom told Dr Nielssen that in December 2008, he and Karlie went for a drive to go sightseeing, have a good time and get him away from drugs. They'd left Khandalyce behind with his cousin in Canberra, taken the Hume Highway north and turned off into the Belanglo State Forest to have a bit of quiet time. Holdom said he and Karlie had just finished having sex when he snapped.

'I can't remember exactly what she has said,' Holdom told the psychiatrist. 'She has threatened to tell my ex Hazel something … that we had an affair in Alice Springs before the car accident …'

Holdom grabbed a broom handle that was being used to prop up the tailgate of Karlie's car and swung it against her rib cage.

'She started vomiting blood and I panicked and took off,' he said.

Holdom claimed Karlie was alive when he left her at the end of the fire trail that morning, but he saw the blood and knew she 'was not in a good way'.

'I had that many drugs in me and I was not thinking straight.'

The obvious omission was the photographs; how did Holdom explain taking the photos of Karlie's body if he took off when she was still alive?

He'd attributed Karlie's death to a serious assault carried out in a haze of ecstasy and methamphetamine, and when his mindset was muddled by grief and torment following the fatal car crash.

As for stealing money from Karlie's account, he claimed he'd blown the money on drugs, living expenses, and support for Hazel and Lauryn.

He knew he'd get caught eventually. 'I have always done things knowing I was going to get caught'.

Justice Hulme was unimpressed. 'He has chosen not to tell me why he killed Karlie and Khandalyce.'

There was a sense that the psychiatric assessment may have been a lost opportunity. Were there follow-up questions that could have been asked or details pressed? Holdom was the only witness to his crimes, the only person who knew exactly what happened in the final minutes of Karlie's and Khandalyce's lives.

In retrospect, it had been the one opportunity to squeeze the truth from him. However, given his effortless history of being untruthful, if he had given a reason for the murders there was no guarantee that what he said would have been true.

Justice Hulme set a sentencing date for November, leaving himself a longer than usual time period to assess the defence and prosecution submissions.

'This is not a straightforward case, from my point of view,' he said.

Chapter 35

At two minutes to 10 am, there were only a few spare seats left in court 5 of the King Street Supreme Court. The rows in the public gallery were filled with family members who had travelled from around the country to be in Sydney for judgement day — Ray and Nick Bell, Karlie's cousin and best friend Samantha Harris and her mother Sharon Harris, other cousins, aunties and uncles. They far outnumbered the two Holdom supporters who quietly walked into the courtroom with a few seconds to spare and sat on a bench seat closest to the dock.

A dozen detectives, all with matching navy, grey and yellow striped ties sporting the Homicide Squad emblem, were seated in the back rows. Journalists squeezed into the jury box and curious lawyers stood at the back of the room.

There was a sense of anticipation and finality inside the courtroom, its dark green walls and giant crest above the bench steeped in history. The King Street court complex is an imposing Georgian, colonial-era building, squeezed in between St James Church and Hyde Park. Built in the 1820s by convicts, it is a heritage listed, sandstone building and one of the few surviving works of Australia's first architects. Stepping into the King Street courthouse feels like stepping into a bygone era.

At 10 am on the dot, a collective hush settled over the crowded courtroom as Justice Hulme walked in. He had his twenty-five-page judgement ready to go, but there had been a late change that threatened to delay the entire sentencing hearing. Minutes before Holdom was to learn his fate, he'd told his solicitor, Ms Fahd, that he wanted to withdraw his guilty plea to the murder of Khandalyce.

It had been four months since he'd admitted to killing Khandalyce and Karlie. Since then he'd told Dr Nielssen how he'd murdered both of them, and had faced a day-long court hearing where his own barrister spoke on his behalf about his guilt. The fact that he had waited until a couple of minutes before the sentence was to be handed down spoke volumes about the sincerity of his argument.

Holdom's junior defence barrister, Thomas Woods, stood and began to tell the judge about Holdom's decision, careful to emphasise that he was relaying his client's instructions. Holdom had been in segregation in jail and had not had access to the full brief of evidence. As a result he hadn't properly had a chance to review what police claimed he did in killing Khandalyce, and he wanted to change his plea.

It was a cowardly and desperate attempt to delay the inevitable.

From their viewing room in Darwin, Scott and Brenda shook their heads in disbelief and swore under their breath. In the courtroom, Karlie and Khandalyce's family were furious and disgusted but remained stoic. Nick Bell, seated less than two metres away from Holdom, barely took his eyes off him.

Justice Hulme pointed out that Holdom had had the prior four months to look at the evidence and assess his plea, but granted Mr Woods a half-hour adjournment to confer with his client. Withdrawing a plea of guilty is extremely rare and only done in limited circumstances — if a defendant could prove the admission did not arise from a genuine appreciation of guilt, or that it was not a deliberate or informed choice. Holdom's legal team had no time to prepare an argument in support of his sudden change of heart and the chance of the application going in his favour was slim to none.

Outside court in the warm spring sun, Karlie and Khandalyce's family fumed over Holdom's delay tactics. They'd all taken time off work and travelled from as far as Alice Springs to be there. After ten years, they were anxious to see justice done.

Just before 11 am, the court resumed and Mr Woods sprang to his feet, appearing slightly more informed. Holdom had not had an opportunity to digest certain aspects of the brief because he had been in segregation, away from the general prison population and his ordinary cell. He disputed certain allegations the police had made and there was a question as to whether Holdom had a genuine consciousness of guilt when it came to the murder of Khandalyce. This, Mr Woods argued, justified the sentence being adjourned so Holdom could pursue his plea-withdrawal application.

Holdom was holding several handwritten notes that explained his dramatic change of mind. Mr Woods offered to have the notes tendered so Justice Hulme could read them while he considered Holdom's argument, but Mr Tedeschi objected: unless Holdom agreed to get in the witness box and be cross-examined on his thought process, the Crown would not agree to the letter being admitted into evidence.

It was a smart move by the prosecution. In the dock, Holdom came across as nervy and easily agitated, not someone who would easily withstand a grilling on the stand.

Ms Fahd walked to the dock and in hushed tones, asked Holdom if he would give evidence. The courtroom was deathly quiet and all eyes were locked on the barely audible but urgent conversation unfolding between the solicitor and her client. It was impossible to hear what was being said but clearly Holdom was reluctant to get up and talk in front of a room full of people, most of whom despised him.

For at least one minute, the judgement and the future of the hearing hung on that conversation.

Ms Fahd returned to the bar table and whispered Holdom's instructions to Mr Woods.

'Your Honour, Holdom is not prepared to be cross-examined about the letter so I cannot take it any further,' he said.

Justice Hulme held firm. 'The application is refused and I will proceed to sentence,' he said.

Without drawing a breath he seamlessly transitioned into reading his judgement as a collective sigh of relief swept across the room.

Justice Hulme chronicled every minute detail of Holdom's crimes: the discovery of Karlie's body, the photographs, the incriminating mobile phone records, the confessions to ex-girlfriends, Khandalyce's suffocation, the missing person's report and the breakthrough Crime Stoppers call.

Karlie and Khandalyce's family were 'cruelly given to think that they were alive' and it gave rise to the torment and despair of not knowing where the mother and daughter were. To some extent, that grew into anger because Karlie hadn't come home or returned her dying mother's calls. The lies Holdom had told in an attempt to justify his actions or cover his tracks had only compounded their grief.

While other judges and magistrates in the past had accepted the links Holdom drew between his criminality and his tough childhood, Justice Hulme did not. The judge was highly critical of the information Holdom had provided in his interview with Dr Nielssen and challenged the psychiatrist's findings.

Holdom had claimed Karlie died in the Belanglo State Forest after he hit her over the rib cage with a broom handle and left her bleeding to death. However, it was 'almost impossible to conceive' Karlie's fatal injuries were inflicted that way, Hulme said, given they were consistent with being stomped on or kneed in the chest. Also, the photographs of Karlie's dead body on Holdom's SD card, didn't show any blood on her.

'Not only are the offender's accounts inaccurate, they are also grossly deficient in explaining truthfully why he did what he did,' Justice Hulme said.

Hulme had pored over pages of school report cards, child welfare reports and jail rehabilitation notes to pick instances where Holdom's evidence didn't add up with records. Yes, his childhood — at least until the age of eight or nine — had been abusive and neglectful, but the consequences of it were in dispute. Holdom — a self-professed bully — claimed his school life suffered; he was kicked out in Year 7 and had a turbulent time in foster care. But teachers in Years 7 and 8 described him as a 'very cooperative student who always tried to please'. Foster carers reported that his behaviour had 'improved remarkably'; he was 'very happy' and well liked. His family's history of PTSD, schizophrenia and personality disorders, as told to Dr Nielssen, also wasn't backed up by independent evidence.

His constant dishonesty, coupled with the frauds carried out in Karlie's name after her murder, and the use of her mobile phone to feign her existence, pointed to a man 'capable of deceiving others when it served his purpose'.

The *Crimes (Sentencing Procedures) Act 1999* (NSW) states a court is to impose a life sentence if the level of culpability is so extreme that community interest in retribution, punishment, protection and deterrence can only be met by keeping a criminal behind bars for life. Subjective circumstances can save a criminal from a life sentence and Holdom may have had two: the atrocious abuse he'd suffered as a child and his plea of guilty.

However, while Justice Hulme acknowledged that Holdom had been abused as a child, he rejected Dr Nielssen's assessment that his childhood 'obviously' contributed to him carrying out the murders. 'It is contended by the defence and not disputed by the Crown that the offender suffered an abusive and neglectful upbringing,' the judge said. 'His stepfather was an alcohol-abusing, brutal and uncaring man who physically and emotionally abused [Daniel Holdom] from the time he was three or four years of age.' It was possible Holdom's upbringing had played a role in shaping the course of his life and might have rendered him more susceptible to depression or an imbalance in his moral compass. 'That is about as much weight as may be given to this subject,' Justice Hulme said.

From the dock, Holdom appeared insulted. He shook his head and glanced at his solicitor, as if willing her to do something. He tapped his fingers on the side of the dock mindlessly.

After forty-five minutes, Justice Hulme began his scathing assessment of the crimes as the public gallery held its breath in anticipation of the sentence. While the Crown had argued for a life sentence, it inevitably came down to the judge to decide the appropriate penalty, including whether Holdom should be indulged with a discount for his guilty plea.

'I accept completely the Crown submission that the last moments of Karlie's life must have been horrendous,' Justice Hulme said. 'She was physically separated from her child, alone in an isolated location in a forest with a man she had trusted and had romantic feelings for. He was a man of considerable height, size and weight, whereas Karlie was described as being of childlike stature. She was killed brutally, most likely by the infliction of severe blunt trauma by the offender either stomping or dropping his knees on her chest and throat region.'

Karlie's indignity was compounded when Holdom violated her in a 'most callous and sadistic way' by sexually assaulting her and taking photographs of his 'unspeakable mistreatment'. He kept those images as a vile trophy of his own inhumanity, Justice Hulme said.

'The final indignity inflicted by the offender was to abandon the body, half-naked, in the forest,' he continued. 'Karlie's remains were not discovered for almost two years and it was not possible to identify them for a further five years.

'The combined force of all of the circumstances point unequivocally to the offender having had nothing less than an intention to kill Karlie. His treatment of her showed complete disdain for her existence as a human being. To him she was just flesh with a life that could be extinguished for his vile pleasure.'

As for what motivated Holdom to kill Karlie, and whether it was to gain access to Khandalyce, for financial gain, a thrill kill, or purely sexually motivated, Justice Hulme was not satisfied that there was proof beyond reasonable doubt.

It was difficult to know what Holdom had been thinking before he murdered Karlie, or whether the fraud and the killing of Khandalyce were afterthoughts. The family would probably never know because Holdom had not explained why he did what he did. However, even without an established motive, Justice Hulme said Karlie's murder amounted to 'extreme gravity and appalling depravity' that put the crime at the top range of objective seriousness.

He turned to Khandalyce's murder. 'What precisely the offender did in killing Khandalyce is unable to be completely determined because of the circumstances in which he did so and the manner in which he disposed of her body,' Justice Hulme said. 'If she was conscious when her mouth was stuffed with dishcloth and duct tape wrapped around her head, her death must have been attended by significant suffering before she passed in[to] unconsciousness.'

No matter how many times the details of Khandalyce's murder were reported in the media or read out during formalities in the courtroom, it was as shocking as hearing them for the first time. Family members shook their heads and glared at Holdom, who fidgeted with the corners of a plastic folder as Justice Hulme addressed the unknown details of Khandalyce's last moments alive.

There was a sexual aspect to her murder, but it was impossible to know how far Holdom got. As the only person who had the answer, he was not a credible witness, and Khandalyce's remains were too degraded to reveal the truth. Holdom was at least trying to or planning to sexually assault the toddler when she died, and that was as far as the court could take it.

'Given this, it is difficult to think why, when she would have been unable to resist him, he would not have gone ahead and done so,' Justice Hulme reasoned. 'But whether he in fact did is indeterminable.'

Her murder was likely prompted by Holdom's need to cover up Karlie's death and turning up in South Australia with the child and not her mother would have been difficult to explain.

'If this was no part of his motive, then he must have killed the child because she was a hindrance to him,' Justice Hulme said. 'Worse explanations for his conduct easily come to mind but must not be asked because of the requirement of proof beyond reasonable doubt.

'This murder is also at the top of the range of objective seriousness. That is so, even if only on the bare fact that the victim was a completely defenceless two year old who was intentionally killed, with some forethought, by being suffocated and stuffed in a suitcase and dumped. Adding to this the sexual assault element only makes it the more despicable.'

After summing up the evidence, Justice Hulme found that Holdom's level of culpability was so extreme and the crimes so heinous that nothing mitigated the need for a life sentence.

'For the murder of Karlie Jade Pearce-Stevenson the offender is sentenced to imprisonment for life,' Justice Hulme ordered as excitable whispers rippled across the court. 'For the murder of Khandalyce Kiara Pearce the offender is sentenced to imprisonment for life.'

Holdom, the sleeves of his jumper pushed up to his elbows, was standing in the dock. He clasped his hands in front of him, turned towards the bench, and barely flinched as he learned he would die in jail.

Triumphant applause broke out in the court as prison officers stepped into the dock and led Holdom to the narrow stairs that descended to the cells beneath.

'Enjoy,' a smirking Nick quipped as the top of Holdom's head disappeared below the courtroom floor.

As family members and detectives filed out of the courtroom, they congratulated one another on the result. Anything less than life in prison would not have been enough in their eyes.

Detective Superintendent Scott Cook introduced himself as the head of the Homicide Squad to Karlie's cousins, aunts and uncles. Rarely did squad commanders turn up to court cases. There was barely enough room in the narrow hallway as journalists squeezed past to join a growing media contingent waiting outside the court. Karlie and Khandalyce's family were private people; they did their best to keep out of the spotlight. In a bid to balance their request for privacy and satisfy the media, the police and the family struck an agreement.

Detective Cook would provide a short statement; the family could stand with him if they wanted, and the cameramen and photographers would not follow them once they left the courthouse, as is a common but intimidating practice in the world of court reporting. A court sheriff secured a gentlemen's agreement from the thirty-odd journalists outside before detectives Cook and Gunn and the family emerged from the courthouse.

'Before we do anything else I would like to acknowledge the family of Karlie and Khandalyce,' Detective Cook said before a wall of microphones. 'They have been stalwarts over the last ten years, they have suffered enormously for the last ten years. They have always conducted themselves with dignity and always assisted the police with the investigation. I would like to congratulate them on that. I hope today brings some conclusion to the trauma they have been through.

'As you know this investigation has been conducted over about 1100 kilometres, four states involving many police from many jurisdictions. I would like to congratulate and thank our partner agencies in the Northern Territory, South Australia and the ACT.

'Finally I would like to congratulate the investigation team led by Detective Sergeant Gunn, who found the person responsible for this matter and brought them before the courts. It is outstanding police work and outstanding cooperation with partner agencies and a good result for the community. Thank you.'

The dozen homicide detectives who had worked on the case celebrated with beers and a meal at The Malaya — a restaurant overlooking Darling Harbour that had become an age-old haunt for the city's detectives to share war stories over chilli chicken wings.

Given Holdom's last-minute attempt to change his plea, detectives and Karlie and Khandalyce's family suspected an appeal against the severity of Holdom's sentence and his conviction was almost inevitable. Holdom had played his hand — he was not ready to concede to a life behind bars or end his victims' family's anguish.

Regardless, Karlie and Khandalyce's relatives walked away from the King Street courthouse with their heads held high as

Scott Povey and Bruce Pearce released a statement on behalf of their family. Michael O'Connell, who had stood aside as South Australia's Victims' Rights Commissioner and was acting on his own as a victims' advocate, had helped Scott and Bruce craft and release the statement. The fact Mr O'Connell, a softly spoken, former police officer who believed strongly in the social value of his work, continued to support them in his own time was a testament to their relationship.

'Today is an important milestone on the heartbreaking and daunting journey on which we were thrust due to Daniel Holdom's despicable crimes,' the statement read. 'We would like to thank the New South Wales Department of Justice for fighting for justice for Karlie, Khandalyce, and us.

'We feared justice for our loved ones would never be attained but Department of Justice staff did not give up. They could not have done more to make amends for what has happened. They have restored our faith in the system, which we worried might not hold Daniel Holdom accountable.

'No sentence will ever bring closure. He murdered a young mother and her child. He stole their whole lives from them and from us. We live daily without Karlie and Khandalyce and will do so for the rest of our lives. His brutality will haunt us forever. Nothing done to him will bring Karlie and Khandalyce back or repay the toll on us.

'Such said, he had forfeited his right to existence. From now until he dies, young women and children must be protected — their safety must be paramount. We do not want another family to suffer as we have.'

Scott and Bruce thanked the investigators in South Australia and New South Wales, particularly Detective Gunn and Detective Paul Ward: 'words seem too little for the gratefulness we have for them'.

They thanked Debbie Gibson, 'the spirit lifter', and the community of Alice Springs; Mr O'Connell for giving the family a voice and for his unwavering presence, and the strangers around Australia who were galvanised by the murders and had rallied around them.

'The best we can say to the mums and dads, grandparents, brothers and sisters and kinfolk is hold your loved ones close and hold them tight and never stop hugging them,' they wrote in their statement.

'We can no longer hold and hug Karlie and Khandalyce but we will never stop loving them.'

Chapter 36

Given Holdom's last-minute attempt to backtrack on his guilty plea, it was no surprise that he began to challenge his life sentence immediately.

In December 2018, he lodged a notice of motion to appeal against the severity of his sentence in the New South Wales Court of Criminal Appeal.

In a series of letters over the past two years and while rotating between Cessnock, Goulburn, Silverwater and Parklea jails, Holdom also attempted to put his voice forward for this book.

He wrote about his childhood, his relationships and the different paths he took in life, all the while careful not to edge too close to addressing the murder charges. Karlie's and Khandalyce's names were not mentioned once.

In January 2018, he outlined his reason for appealing; he didn't agree with what the prosecution said or the entirety of the facts. That was despite him pleading guilty to the lengthy and detailed fact sheet six months earlier.

'What was said does not coincide with the brief of evidence an [sic] it is blatantly clear there is so much,' he wrote.

'Even family and one close friend said you should fight cause that part was not you. This has a very long way to go an [sic] a lot of investigating.'

In a subsequent letter received two weeks later, Holdom finally mentioned Khandalyce's name. He wanted to plead not guilty to her murder and forecast that there would be a trial on that charge.

He suggested there were other people involved in the crime. The list of children's names with the words 'rape' or 'consent' scribbled in a neighbouring column was something Holdom had written to 'have over' someone else, he claimed.

In other words, it wasn't to be taken literally.

He did not address why he made admissions to his psychologists and ex-girlfriends about Khandalyce's murder if he wasn't guilty. 'I know everyone is keen to make me the bad villan [sic] in all this an [sic] I know I made things worse by pleading instead of fighting,' he wrote.

Lastly, Holdom pointed out, Hazel Passmore was not the victim she'd presented herself as, and he picked apart inconsistencies in her induced statement compared to forensic evidence, such as Khandalyce being murdered in Belanglo State Forest rather than Narrandera. Dereck's evidence also had holes in it, Holdom suggested. 'That's why I am confident in my appeal and will be taking to the witness box to clear myself of the worse [sic] of this.'

After settling out of court in her civil suit against Holdom, Hazel had received a hefty sum and moved back to Queensland with her partner and children.

She did not respond to requests for an interview via her barrister.

At the time of publication, a decision was yet to be made on whether Holdom would be granted leave to appeal.

Epilogue

A ceiling fan whirred above Scott Povey as he looked out across one of Darwin's picturesque bays. It was the peak of summer and most people had cleared out of the city in search of cooler weather for the holidays.

Scott didn't mind the empty streets — he'd only recently started venturing outside a close network of friends and family again after a very dark time in his life.

The anxiety that had consumed him post October 2015 had sent him into a self-imposed period of isolation for almost a year. He didn't work and avoided going out in public in case a random encounter with an old friend on the street led to a conversation about his dead daughter and granddaughter.

He'd only recently come good, he explained, after deciding he needed to try and resume a normal life again.

Two weeks earlier had marked the tenth anniversary of Karlie's and Khandalyce's murders. Three weeks prior, the man responsible for the killings was jailed for life. As the harshest sentence available under Australian law, it was the result Scott had hoped for.

But with the court case that hung over his family for three years now over, Scott reflected on what it all meant. There was a softness in the way he carefully chose his words. Despite the subject matter, there was never a hint of anger or malice in his voice.

As he pondered whether it would be more satisfying to see Holdom dead or alive, it was clear he had thought about the question deeply. 'For instant gratification yes but … to see him suffer and suffer, I can't change that,' he said.

'If someone pulled the trigger or the trap door I'd be the first one there. But it wouldn't be enough because it puts him out of his misery. In many ways I'd rather see him stay alive, I really would.'

Like Scott, Tanya has been through torturous periods of blaming herself. She wondered whether she did enough to help Karlie and Khandalyce and whether she missed any blatant warning signs.

The phone call with Karlie the week before her death haunts her especially. If Tanya had intervened would it have put Karlie and Khandalyce on a different path? At the very least, it might have meant their bodies weren't left discarded in desolate locations for two and seven years.

Colleen didn't live long enough to find out what happened to her daughter and granddaughter and Tanya's glad for it. If Colleen had known what Karlie and Khandalyce had gone through, it would've killed her.

'I don't think she would have been able to deal with that,' she reflected after the sentencing. 'What mother would?'

Tanya remains close to Scott and Luke, not only because she sees them as family but because she made a promise to her best friend before she died.

The words, uttered by Colleen from her bed in the palliative care unit, will forever be etched in her memory.

'She said, "can you look after Luke and can you find Karlie?"' Tanya remembered through tears. Dabbing a tissue under her eyes she chuckled awkwardly: 'I told myself I wouldn't cry.'

It was clear the burden of Colleen's final request weighed heavily on Tanya and, at times, she felt like she'd failed her. But the self-blame was misplaced. Tanya's loyalty and love for her dear friend meant she never stopped looking for Karlie.

She helped the family bring Karlie and Khandalyce home, where they were buried beside Colleen and with Connie's ashes in the Alice Springs Garden Cemetery. The headstone reads: 'In our hearts and each other's arms forever'.

Author's Note

Content for this book was collected from a range of sources, including historical court files, court hearings, welfare records, medical reports and through interviews with friends, relatives, investigators and experts.

Given the passage of time, people's memories of certain events or conversations varied. Sometimes these versions of events were supported by other material, such as old emails or official records.

Where information was based on one person's memory, I have made that clear.

Due to the nature of this case, some accounts provided were self-serving and had to be treated very carefully.

I have strived to accurately reflect the events of the past ten years by taking into account many different versions, recollections and opinions.

References

Chapter 4

R v Milat & Klein (2012) NSWSC 634, NSW Caselaw,
viewed 1 November 2018, www.caselaw.nsw.gov.au/decisi
on/54a637ad3004de94513d9a99

Chapter 6

Australian Bureau of Statistics 2016, *Census Quickstats —
Wynarka*, viewed December 8 2018, quickstats.censusdata.
abs.gov.au/census_services/getproduct/census/2016/
quickstat/SSC41647

Place names of South Australia — W, The Manning Index
of South Australian History, viewed 18 November 2018,
www.slsa.sa.gov.au/manning/pn/w/w10.htm#wynarka

Chapter 7

National Pathology Accreditation Advisory Council,
2018, *Requirements for The Retention of Laboratory Records
and Diagnostic Material*, ed. 7, accessed 10 December 2018,
www.health.gov.au

Bowman, D & Studdert D, 2011, 'Newborn screening
cards: a legal quagmire', *The Medical Journal of Australia*,

vol. 194, no. 6, *www.mja.com.au/journal/2011/194/6/ newborn-screening-cards-legal-quagmire*

Chapter 9
Australian Bureau of Statistics 2016, *Census Quickstats — Alice Springs*, accessed 8 December 2018, quickstats. censusdata.abs.gov.au/census_services/getproduct/ census/2016/quickstat/LGA70200

Chapter 23
Williams, B, February 2015, 'Homicide', *Police Journal*, pages 10–21, viewed 14 February 2018, issuu.com/ policeassociationsa/docs/policejournal_february2015_5

Chapter 34
Spigleman, CJ, 2009, *Swearing in ceremony of The Honourable Robert Allan Hulme*, accessed 8 December 2018, classic. austlii.edu.au/au/journals/NSWJSchol/2009/5

Chapter 35
NSW Office of Environment and Heritage, 2010, *Sydney Supreme Courthouse (Old Supreme Court)*, accessed 10 December 2018, www.environment.nsw.gov.au/ heritageapp/ViewHeritageItemDetails.aspx?ID=3080013

Acknowledgements

Dozens of people from around the country spoke with me as part of this book, including a knowledgeable few off the record.

To the anonymous sources who went out of their way to help me piece this case together, thank you. I am extremely grateful to my employers and colleagues at *The Sunday Telegraph* for affording me the time and support to juggle this project. Thank you to my publisher, Jude McGee, and ABC Books for backing me from the outset and guiding me through this unchartered territory, Ainslie Blackstone, New South Wales Police and the media team at the New South Wales Department of Justice.

Thank you to my dear friends Ashleigh and Hannah for living the deadlines with me, Emma for always picking up the phone to offer reassuring advice, Jack for your patience and sharp eye and my family, Lisa, Peter and Lily, for your love and encouragement.

Finally, I'd like to acknowledge the friends and family of Karlie Pearce-Stevenson and Khandalyce. For reasons that will never be clear, you have been forced to suffer unimaginable grief and loss. Yet you kindly opened your homes and shared your precious and, at times, painful, memories with me. I am grateful for your trust and in awe of your strength.